Churchill

Churchill
David Mason

BB

Editor-in-Chief: Barrie Pitt
Editor: David Mason
Art Director: Sarah Kingham
Picture Editor: Robert Hunt
Consultant Art Editor: Denis Piper
Designer: David Allen
Illustration: John Batchelor
Photographic Research: Carina Dvorak/ Jonathan Moore
Cartographer: Richard Natkiel

Photographs for this book were especially selected from the following archives: from left to right page 2 Imperial War Museum, London; 2 US Army, Washington; 2 Popperfotos, London; 2-3 IWM; 8-9 Popperfoto; 10 US National Archives, Washington; 10 Bundesarchiv, Koblenz; 11 National Archives; 11 Topix, London; 12 Keystone Press Agency, London; · 14-15 National Archives; 16 Associated Press, London; 17 IWM; 18-19 Alfredo Zennaro, Rome; 20-21 United Press International, London; 22 IWM; 22 National Archives; 24 Czechoslovak News Agency, Prague; 24 National Archives; 25 Popperfoto; 26-27 Czech News Agency; 32-33 National Archives; 33 Keystone; 24 IWM; 36 US Navy; 37-41 IWM; 42-43 Sado-Opera Mundi, Belgium; 44-50 IWM; 50-51 Keystone; 54 Popperfoto; 55 IWM; 55 National Archives; 56-57 IWM; 58 Keystone; 60 National Archives; 62-69 IWM; 70 Bundesarchiv; 71 Suddeutscher Verlag, Munich; 72-73 Bundesarchiv; 74-75 IWM; 76 UPI; 77-89 IWM; 90 National Archives; 91 Bundesarchiv; 92 IWM; 92 Bundesarchiv; 93-95 IWM; 96-97 National Archives; 98-101 IWM; 103 Keystone; 104 IWM; 106 Bundesarchiv; 107 Fujipotos, Tokyo; 108-109 Sado-Opera Mundi; 110-111 IWM; 110 Keystone; 111 National Archives; 113-119 IWM; 120 Etablissement Cinematographique et Photographique des Armees, France; 120-124 IWM; 125 US Army; 126-138 IWM; 138 US Army; 139-149 IWM; 150 Black Star Publishing Co, London; 151 IWM; 152 Ballantine; 156 Keystone; 156 IWM; 157 US Army; 158 Popperfoto.
Front cover The Economist, London; Back cover Imperial War Museum, London
Extracts from speeches in the House of Commons are printed
by permission of the Controller, Her Majesty's Stationery Office, London. The author gratefully
acknowledges permission granted by the authors and publishers concerned to quote from the following books:
Th Second World War by Winston Churchill, Cassells (London), Houghton Mifflin Company (Boston)
The White House Papers by R Sherwood, Eyre & Spottiswoode (London)
A Thread in the Tapestry by Sarah Churchill, Andre Deutsch (London), Dodd Mead & Co, Inc (New York)
The War that Churchill Waged by Lewis Broad, Hutchinson (London and New York)
Winston Churchill, The Struggle for Survival 1940-1965 by Lord Moran, Constable & Co (London)

First Printing: **December** 1972
Printed in United States of America

Ballantine Books Inc.
101 Fifth Avenue New York NY10003

An Intext Publisher

Contents

'The Greatest Living Englishman'

Introduction by Barrie Pitt

When, at one of the early reunions of the veterans of the Eighth Army, Field-Marshal Viscount Montgomery of Alamein referred to Churchill in such terms there was no serious dispute about the validity of the claim – apart, of course, from the snide comments of his political and private enemies.

Since those days, however, there have been several analytical and well-considered studies of the events with which Churchill was most intimately concerned, and the conclusions to be drawn from them indicate that he was mistaken in many of his beliefs, headstrong in many of his actions, childish in many of his reactions, tortuous in many of his dealings and misguided in several of his decisions.

Yet he remains indisputably the greatest Englishman of our time. Why?

How can one explain this apparent enigma, especially when it contains a further enigma in the distinct possibility that no explanation is required of an obvious and indestructible fact?

But history requires that an attempt be made and many vain and frustrating hours have been spent attempting to grasp the heart of the mystery and explain it in simple and comprehensible terms. One might as easily describe the inscrutability of Buddha. For-

tunately, however, if explanation is impossible, demonstration is comparatively easy, for Churchill's power rang in his speeches and of these we have ample record. Churchill's secret is most clearly recorded in Churchill's own words.

'I do not grudge our loyal, brave people who were ready to do their duty no matter what the cost . . . the natural, spontaneous outburst of joy and relief when they learned that the hard ordeal would no longer be required of them at the moment; but they should know the truth. They should know that there had been gross neglect and deficiency in our defences; they should know that we have sustained a defeat without a war, the consequences of which will travel far with us along our road; they should know that we have passed an awful milestone in our history, when the whole equilibrium of Europe has been deranged, and that the terrible words have for the time being been pronounced against the Western democracies: "Thou art weighed in the balance and found wanting". And do not suppose that this is the end. This is only the beginning of the reckoning. This is only the first sip, the first foretaste of a bitter cup which will be proffered to us year by year unless, by a supreme recovery of moral health and martial vigour, we arise again and take our stand for freedom as in the olden times.'

'. . . as I went to bed at about 3 a.m. I was conscious of a profound sense of relief. At last I had the authority to give directions over the whole scene. I felt as if I were walking with destiny, and that all my past life had been but a preparation for this hour and for this trial.'

'I would say to the House, as I said to those who have joined this government: I have nothing to offer but blood, toil, tears and sweat ... You ask, What is our policy? I will say: it is to wage war by sea, land, and air, with all our might and with all the strength that God can give us; to wage war against a monstrous tyranny, never surpassed in the dark, lamentable catalogue of human crime. That is our policy. You ask, what is our aim? I can answer in one word. It is victory, victory at all costs, victory in spite of all terror, victory however long and hard the road may be – for without victory there is no survival.'

'Even though large tracts of Europe and many old and famous States have fallen or may fall into the grip of the Gestapo and all the odious apparatus of Nazi rule, we shall not flag or fail. We shall go on to the end. We shall fight in France, we shall fight in the seas and oceans, we shall fight with growing confidence and growing strength in the air; we shall defend our Island whatever the cost may be. We shall fight on the beaches, we shall fight on the landing-grounds, we shall fight in the fields and in the streets, we shall fight in the hills; we shall never surrender; and even if, which I do not for a moment believe, this Island or a large part of it were subjugated and starving, then our Empire beyond the seas, armed and guarded by the British Fleet, would carry on the struggle, until, in God's good time, the New World, with all its power and might, steps forth to the rescue and liberation of the Old.'

'The Battle of France is over. The Battle of Britain is about to begin. Upon it depends our way of life. The whole fury and weight of the enemy must very soon be turned on us. If we fail, the whole world will sink into an abyss of a new dark age, made more sinister, and perhaps more protracted, by the lights of a perverted science. Let us therefore brace ourselves to our duties and so bear ourselves that, if the British Empire and Commonwealth last for a thousand years, men will still say: "This was their finest hour".'

Against such stature, his human frailties were miniscule.

Out of the Wilderness

Winston Churchill became Prime Minister of Great Britain on 10th May 1940. He took office in the middle of, and largely as a result of, the crisis in the European situation which marked the end of the so-called 'phoney war'. This was the period when the German military machine carried out its explosive expansion into Scandinavia and the Low Countries, when France was invaded, and when Hitler's armies threatened to invade Britain itself. It was the point at which Europe was plunged irrevocably into total war. And it was for Churchill the beginning of a five-year period during which he ran the civil, political and military organisations of his country with a command and authority which no other politician has ever been able to achieve. So far as Britain was concerned, and to a great extent so far as the rest of the free world was concerned, the first one or two years of that five-year period were indisputably Churchill's years, and it was on 10th May 1940 that they began.

Nevertheless, Churchill's concern with the Second World War had begun more than two decades before hostilities opened, when he first began to recognise the implications of international developments, and the inadequacies of the policies then being pursued to deal with them. His views at this time were considered eccentric, dangerous and outdated, and he was subjected to a campaign of abuse and vilification which included accusations of 'scaremongering' and 'warmongering'. The condemnation of Churchill was almost universal, yet

Prime Minister Churchill speaks in London, July 1941

9

Above: Nucleus of the new German Army: troops parade through Munich in 1921. *Below:* General Hans Von Seekt

his views can be seen, in the light of subsequent history, to have been soundly based on an almost uncannily accurate reading of the disturbing developments in European affairs.

Churchill's analysis of the new threat to peace in Europe was prompted by two separate developments in Germany during the 1920s; the resurgence of German military power and the growing political strength of the Nazi party.

From the early years after the end of the First World War Germany, in defiance of the Versailles Treaty, was engaged in a vigorous though largely secret rearmament programme. During the 1920s General von Seeckt was busy building up the nucleus of a German army, training a corps of staff officers for the future, and forcing them to abandon the out-of-date concepts of the previous war and to think in terms of entirely new principles, notably the integration and tactical cooperation of all arms – artillery, infantry, cavalry, and even air squadrons.

At the same time Adolf Hitler was gaining power. Having taken over the leadership of the German Workers' Party, soon to become the National Socialist Party, he spent a brief

Adolf Hitler, dominant figure in the
awakening Nazi party

period in prison during which he
devoted himself to the preparation of
the political treatise *Mein Kampf*,
in which he expressed all the ideas of
racial purity and militant nationalism
which, seen in conjunction with the
other developments then taking place,
could lead in one direction only.

In this gloomy combination of
circumstances – Germany rearming
and Hitler in firm control of his country and with his views and intentions
declared – the danger to peace might
be thought to have been obvious to
every intelligent observer. Perhaps it
was, but there were conflicting views,
in Britain at least, about how the
threat should be answered. The
government in office during the early
1930s, an uneasy coalition of Conservatives and Liberals presided over
by the former Labour leader Ramsay
MacDonald, was overwhelmingly in
favour of disarmament as a means of
countering the German menace. Not
only were they prompted by the
financial climate to try to reduce the
level of armaments held by the Allies,
but at the same time they subscribed
to a political philosophy of 'fair play'

Ramsay MacDonald, first of the British
Prime Ministers who pursued policies
of conciliation towards Nazi Germany

11

Winston Churchill's library, showing a model of Port Arromanches, the artificial harbour used much later in his story, on D-Day

Winston's study, the base for his campaign against German rearmament

which held that it was only right for the country defeated in the previous conflict to hold the same level of armaments as the victors. There was little opposition to this view. Almost everybody, it seemed, was prepared to acquiesce in the growth of a militantly nationalistic and militarily powerful Germany. Almost everybody, that is, except Winston Churchill.

As early as 1928 he envisaged, in his book *The Aftermath*, the awesome possibilities offered by the new weapons which had begun to show their potential in 1918. He also, writing only ten years after the end of the First World War and more than ten years before the beginning of the Second World War, suggested with great accuracy of perception that Europe had entered on 'that period of exhaustion which has been described as Peace'.

In May 1932 Churchill gave the first of a long series of warnings in the House of Commons of the dangers that lay ahead, when he expressed his fears at the prospects of an approximation of military strength between Germany and France. 'For my part,' he warned, 'I earnestly hope that no such approximation will take place during my lifetime or that of my children. To say that is not in the least to imply any want of regard or admiration for the great qualities of the German people, but I am sure that the thesis that they should be placed in an equal military position with France is one which, if it ever emerged in fact, would bring us within practical distance of almost measureless calamity.'

Less than a year later, on 14th March 1933, he returned to the subject during a debate on the British air estimates when he expressed his regret at Britain's relegation to fifth place as an air power, and his dismay at the Air Ministry's boast that they had not laid down a single new unit that year. 'We should be well advised', he told the House, 'to con-centrate upon our air defences with greater vigour.'

Only one week after the air estimates debate, on 23rd March, Churchill again pressed his views in Parliament: 'When we read about Germany, when we watch with surprise and distress the tumultuous insurgence of ferocity and war spirit, the pitiless ill-treatment of minorities, the denial of the normal protections of civilised society, the persecution of large numbers of individuals solely on the ground of race – when we see all that occurring in one of the most gifted, learned, and scientific and formidable nations in the world, one cannot help feeling glad that the fierce passions that are raging in Germany have not yet found any other outlet but upon themselves.'

And in April, again in Parliament, he spelled out his warning in greater detail: '. . . as surely as Germany acquires full military equality with her neighbours while her own grievances are still unredressed and while she is in the temper which we have unhappily seen, so surely shall we see ourselves within a measurable distance of the renewal of general European war.'

As Churchill continued to expound his views in this vein during the years leading up to the war, he gradually found himself attracting the support of small numbers of like-minded individuals. Within Parliament, he became the leader of a group of members who, although not in the cabinet, were experienced and widely respected. Outside Parliament, to help him in his campaign, he gathered around him a nucleus of expert advisers who held positions, some of them in the intelligence services and the Foreign Office, from which they could supply Churchill with invaluable information. There were also associated with his circle small numbers of important figures from all parts of Europe, notably French political leaders and German anti-Nazis, who added their views and information to Churchill's own.

Churchill during these years spent the greater part of his time at Chartwell, his home in Kent some twenty miles from London. He had bought this large, appealing, but architecturally undistinguished mansion in 1922 from the proceeds of his writing, and the house was to become, during the decade when he held no government office, the centre for his fight against the menace of German rearmament. Here he received a steady stream of visitors, influential and knowledgeable men, and here he collected the information and amassed the facts on which he based his campaign. Because of his unique combination of years of experience of high office, familiarity from previous years with 'state secrets', and current political independence, Churchill was able to build up a body of knowledge which few men, even members of the Government, could rival; and Chartwell, and especially the famous study in which he worked and wrote, was likened by some observers to a miniature Foreign Office.

Early in 1934 he again spoke against the British government's policy of working for the disarmament of France. He warned that if Britain were not in a proper state of security they might be faced with a 'visit from an Ambassador' such as had drawn France into war in 1914, and that following such a visit 'within the next few hours the crash of bombs exploding in London and cataracts of masonry and fire and smoke will warn us of any inadequacy which has been permitted in our aerial defences.'

He went on: 'Not one of the lessons of the past has been learned, not one of them has been applied, and the situation is incomparably more dangerous. Then we had the Navy and no air menace. Then the Navy was the 'sure shield' of Britain . . . We

Part of Germany's growing air power, the Horst Wessel fighter squadron at Dortmund in 1936

Stanley Baldwin, successor to Ramsay MacDonald as British Prime Minister

cannot say that now. This cursed, hellish invention and development of war from the air has revolutionised our position. We are not the same kind of country we used to be when we were an island, only twenty years ago.'

In July 1934 a debate took place in the House of Commons following the indefinite adjournment of the Standing Committee of the Disarmament Conference at Geneva, and during it Churchill took the opportunity of expressing his general opinion of the conciliatory approach to politics, and more particularly of the character of the German government. On the first matter he said: 'I am very glad that the Disarmament Conference is passing out of life into history. It is the greatest mistake to mix up disarmament with peace. When you have peace you will have disarmament.' On the second he pointed out 'that at present two or three men, in what may be a desperate position, have the whole of that mighty country in their grip, have that wonderful scientific, intelligent, docile, valiant people in their grip, a population of seventy millions; that there is no dynastic interest such as a monarchy brings as a restraint upon policy . . . and that there is no public opinion except what is manufactured by those new and terrible engines, broadcasting and a controlled Press.' There was, he said, 'more danger in this kind of dictatorship than there would be in a military dicatatorship, because you have men who, to relieve themselves from the great peril which confronts them at home, might easily plunge into a foreign adventure of the most dangerous and catastrophic character to the whole world.'

In that same month, to Churchill's intense satisfaction, the government announced a small number of measures towards rearmament, albeit modest and belated ones, including the addition of forty-one Royal Air Force squadrons totalling 820 aircraft during the next five years. The Labour party reacted immediately, and introduced a censure motion in the House, in which they were backed by the Liberal party, deploring the government's entry upon a policy of rearmament 'certain to jeopardise the prospects of international disarmament and to encourage a revival of dangerous and wasteful competition in preparation for war.'

When Churchill came to make his contribution to the debate, he painted a vivid picture of Britain's position: 'We are a rich and easy prey. No country is so vulnerable, and no country would better repay pillage than our own . . . With our enormous metropolis here, the greatest target in the world, a kind of tremendous, fat, valuable cow tied up to attract the beast of prey, we are in a position in which we have never been before, and in which no other country is at the present time. Let us remember this; our weakness does not only involve ourselves; our weakness involves also the stability of Europe.'

After that burst of colourful rhetoric, Churchill went on to deal with the question of air strength, which he already saw as the true key to conquering the threat of German aggression. He asserted that Germany had already built up an air force two thirds as strong as Britain's, that by 1935 they would have achieved parity, and that by 1936 they would be stronger in the air than Britain.

He returned to this aspect of the problem again in November 1934, when some members of the Parliamentary group of which he was the leading figure moved an amendment to the effect that 'the strength of our national defences and especially of our air defences is no longer adequate to secure the peace, safety, and freedom of Your Majesty's faithful subjects'. In the course of his speech Churchill gave his revised estimates of the developing strength of the respective air forces, pointing out that by 1936 the German air force would be fifty per cent stronger than that of Britain, and by 1937 nearly double the strength.

The House of Commons gave Churchill a ready hearing on this occasion. Many of them by now accepted him as a well-informed expert on the subject, even if they disagreed with his views, but Mr Baldwin, on behalf of the government, completely destroyed the amendment by means of a categorical assertion, which the House was only too pleased to accept, that Churchill's figures were untrue: 'Such investigations as I have been able to make lead me to believe that his figures are considerably exaggerated.'

The issue came under consideration again during the air estimates debate

Professor F A Lindemann with Churchill at a weapons demonstration. Churchill made his friend's appointment to the Committee of Imperial Defence on Air Defence Research a condition of his own appointment

of the following spring, when on 19th March 1935 he repeated his figures, and they were again denied by the government. Shortly after this, however, it was made known publicly that during a recent visit by the Lord Privy Seal and the Foreign Secretary to Berlin, Hitler himself had boasted that Germany had already achieved parity with Britain in air forces. On 22nd May Baldwin openly confessed in the House that the government had been in error in their estimate of developing German strength: 'There I was completely wrong,' he said. 'We were completely misled on that subject.'

Churchill hoped that this extraordinary confession would be decisive, that the government would be forced into action, and that an all-party committee would be set up to examine the facts and report on the nation's safety. But he had misread the situation. Members on both sides were won over by Baldwin's frankness and by his generosity in protecting the Air Minister and shouldering the blame on behalf of the entire government. Nothing was done.

Gradually, however, the climate of opinion in the government was beginning to change. In June, failing health and the bankruptcy of his disarmament policy forced Ramsay MacDonald to give up the post of Prime Minister, and Baldwin took over. A month later Baldwin approached Churchill with an invitation to join the newly formed Committee of Imperial Defence on Air Defence Research, a body whose formation Churchill had been urging for some time. Churchill hestitated only long enough to establish two conditions before agreeing, one that he would remain free to comment critically on the state of air preparedness, the other that his friend and scientific adviser, Professor Lindemann, would be appointed to the technical sub-committee at the same time. The committee began its work almost immediately, so that by the time

war began Churchill was thoroughly familiar with many of the devices, including radar and asdic, which would be brought into use.

In the autumn of 1935, the nation's growing mood of determination was hardened by the Italian invasion of Abyssinia. The pacifist George Lansbury was forced to resign the leadership of the Labour party, and some socialists openly called for action against Italy.

Shortly after the Abyssinian invasion, a general election took place in Britain. Churchill, aware that Britain and France would almost certainly soon have to answer some form of challenge from the European dictators, hoped for and expected office in the new government if the Conservatives were returned to power. He looked forward particularly to the post of First Lord of the Admiralty, where he had served a controversial term of office during the First World War, and which he understood would fall vacant.

'The growing German menace', he wrote in his memoirs, 'made me anxious to lay my hands upon our military machine.'

The Conservatives were indeed returned to power, with a huge clear majority of 247. But Baldwin, with

The Italians enter Abyssinia

such a margin of popularity, could afford to deny public and press opinion, and he pointedly excluded Churchill from the cabinet. It was one of the many lucky events in Churchill's life. He immediately took a holiday, spent the dreariest months of the English winter on and around the Mediterranean, and remained at a safe distance from Westminster while a severe crisis developed over Abyssinia which rocked the government and almost brought the downfall of Baldwin himself.

The early months of 1936 confirmed Churchill's view of the impending course of events in Europe, when on 7th March Hitler's forces occupied the Rhineland. In the debate which followed, rather belatedly, at the end of March, Churchill again with his customary accuracy foresaw that the Rhineland would, when fortified, 'be a barrier across Germany's front door which will leave her free to sally out eastwards and southwards by the other doors'. A week later, during a debate on the government's foreign policy, he took up this theme again, and said in the course of his speech: 'The creation of a line of forts opposite to the French frontier will enable the German troops to be economised on that line, and will enable the main forces to swing round through Belgium and Holland.'

It was during this period that Baldwin delivered to Churchill his second severe rebuff. In response to the growing pressure to take the German threat more seriously Baldwin created a Ministry for the Co-ordination of Defence. It was widely thought that Churchill would be the ideal and natural choice for the job. Churchill did not entirely approve of the form of the new organisation, but he would have been willing to accept the post. His experience in office in the First World War, his insistence on collective security, and his semi-

Churchill goes campaigning in the 1935 general election

Above: A critical event of 1936 : German troops march into the 'demilitarised' zone of the Rhineland ; Churchill accurately recorded its strategic significance. *Below:* The German army occupies Vienna, 1938

official position on the Defence Committee appeared to represent perfect qualifications, and he was moreover free from the responsibilities of any current office. Yet Baldwin again pointedly failed to nominate him. Churchill was as offended and hurt as the press and public were indignant and astonished. Churchill later wrote that Baldwin thought he had dealt him a politically fatal stroke, and Churchill indeed at that time agreed. His isolation was absolute, yet again he kept his composure, ignored his continuing ostracism, and continued to work for his cause. And once more he had the good fortune, though he only later recognised it, to remain detached from the government during the years leading up to the war, and at the beginning of the war to have an untarnished record, with no share of the responsibility for the unprepared condition in which Britain would have to fight it.

Churchill's next major step was to establish, by two exhaustive and efficient private research studies, the extent of German expenditure on armaments. In the spring of 1936 he told Parliament that Germany had spent the sum of two thousand million pounds sterling on armaments in the preceding three years, and that their munitions expenditure was increasing at an alarming rate. Neville Chamberlain, then Chancellor of the Exchequer, replied to the effect that the figures mentioned by Churchill were by no means excessive.

In July 1936 Churchill carried his cause further when, as a member of a deputation of highly respected and influential members of both the House of Commons and the House of Lords, he laid before the Prime Minister the facts as they saw them. Churchill himself made the opening statement of the deputation, in the course of which he told the Prime Minister unequivocally that his country was facing the greatest danger and emergency of its history. He called for the unification of the British navy and the French army and the air forces of the two nations, operating close behind the French and Belgian frontiers as a deterrent. He called for the development of air power by every possible means, and ended with the warning: 'We are in danger, as we have never been in danger before – no, not even at the height of the submarine campaign.'

It might be thought that this powerful delegation, issuing such a powerful warning, and having the willing ear of the Prime Minister and his officials, would have led to vigorous and direct action, however belatedly. But again little happened. Baldwin ceased to be Prime Minister a few months later, and the man who succeeded him, Neville Chamberlain, had not been present to hear the deputation. Churchill and his colleagues had been talking to empty air, and the only result of the meeting was a note from the Minister of Coordination of Defence some months later, to the effect that the estimates of the group took an excessively gloomy view, that emergency measures would only cause alarm, but that within these limitations everything was being done to remedy the situation which it was acknowledged was grave.

The deterioration in Britain's strength, relative to that of the more rapidly arming Germany, continued at a steady pace until the early part of 1938, when both international affairs and national political events in Britain began to move at an increasing rate, culminating on 12th March with the German army's occupation of Vienna. Churchill records that he was 'hit hard' by this outrage, and two days after it he pleaded with the House of Commons not to put off action any longer: '. . . there is only one choice open, not only to us but to other countries, either to submit like Austria, or else take effective measures while time remains to ward off the danger, and if it cannot be warded off to cope with it.'

He also in this speech drew attention to the next crisis which he foresaw

Left : Lord Halifax, Foreign Secretary in Chamberlain's government and preferred to Churchill as his successor.
Below : Chamberlain arrives in Munich for his third meeting with Hitler.
Right : 'Peace for our time'. Chamberlain brings back to London the famous agreement with Hitler

Czechoslovakia falls

would soon follow, when he warned of the perils which now faced the state of Czechoslovakia, isolated in both economic and military terms. His view, of course, proved right, but as he held no office and his opinion carried no effective weight, the position of Czechoslovakia continued to deteriorate. The only politician whose opinion carried any real weight was Chamberlain, who maintained a firm and unyielding personal control of foreign policy. Such indeed was his determination to remain in control that he consulted neither his own Foreign Secretary Lord Halifax, nor the French government who were bound by treaty obligations to Czechoslovakia, nor even the Czechoslovakian government themselves, when he decided on his own initiative to approach Hitler and suggest a meeting between the two of them to discuss the Czechoslovakian question. Hitler accepted, and on 15th September Chamberlain flew to Munich. After conversations with Hitler Chamberlain returned two days later to formulate proposals designed to avert a German invasion by handing over to Germany areas of Czechoslovakia containing more than fifty per cent German population.

Churchill remained unequivocal in his condemnation of the government and its policies. On 21st September he described the proposed partition of Czechoslovakia as a 'complete surrender of the Western Democracies to the Nazi threat of force' which would bring peace and security neither to England nor to France. On the contrary, he pointed out, it would place those two nations in an ever weaker and more dangerous situation, releasing twenty-five German divisions for possible use on the Western front.

Two days later Chamberlain again flew to Germany, where Hitler presented him with an entirely new set of proposals, which both the British and French governments rejected. For a short time it looked as if the war which Churchill had predicted, and to which he looked forward as the only honourable and effective course, was inevitable and imminent. The British navy and the French army were ordered to mobilise. Then a letter arrived from Hitler offering to help guarantee Czechoslovakia's frontiers. Chamberlain responded hopefully to this, and replied offering to meet Hitler yet again in Germany to formulate a settlement which would avoid war.

On 29th September 1938 Chamberlain therefore flew to Germany for the third time, for the famous Munich

meeting, at which the French, Italian, and British leaders agreed with Hitler that the Sudetenland should be evacuated, and that an International Commission should be established to determine the final frontier. These proposals were presented to the Czechoslovakian government as a *fait accompli*. Chamberlain and Hitler also met separately, and produced a declaration in which they resolved to settle all their differences by consultation, and continue their efforts to remove possible sources of difference and thus contribute to the peace of Europe. It was this declaration, bearing Hitler's signature, which Chamberlain waved to the people of London, from a balcony in Downing Street, with the famous proclamation that he had come back from Germany bringing peace with honour, which he believed to be 'peace for our time'.

Churchill, in the House of Commons debate which followed, acknowledged that Chamberlain had been a resolute and uncompromising struggler for peace, but having made that concession, he went on to underline at length the doom which he foresaw this settlement would bring.

'All is over. Silent, mournful, abandoned, broken, Czechoslovakia recedes into the darkness. She has suffered in every respect by her associations with France, under whose guidance and policy she has been actuated for so long . . .

'I find unendurable the sense of our country falling into the power, into the orbit and influence of Nazi Germany, and of our existence becoming dependent upon their goodwill or pleasure. It is to prevent that that I have tried my best to urge the maintenance of every bulwark of defence . . . It has all been in vain. Every position has been successively undermined and abandoned on specious and plausible excuses.

'I do not grudge our loyal, brave people who were ready to do their duty no matter what the cost . . . the natural, spontaneous outburst of joy and relief when they learned that the hard ordeal would no longer be required of them at the moment; but they should know the truth. They should know that there has been gross neglect and deficiency in our defences; they should know that we have sustained a defeat without a war, the consequences of which will travel far with us along our road; they should know that we have passed an awful milestone in our history, when the whole equilibrium of Europe has been deranged, and that the terrible words have for the time being been pronounced against the Western democracies: 'Thou art weighed in the balance and found wanting'. And do not suppose that this is the end. This in only the beginning of the reckoning. This is only the first sip, the first foretaste of a bitter cup which will be proffered to us year by year unless, by a supreme recovery of moral health and martial vigour, we arise again and take our stand for freedom as in the olden times.'

But even this impassioned appeal failed to convert the country to Churchill's views. The predominant feeling, inside Parliament and outside, was that Chamberlain had achieved a masterly feat of diplomacy in averting war, and those MPs who failed to support him in the vote at the end of the debate were widely attacked. Churchill faced a personal political crisis in his own constituency, where his local party association, on whose support any British member of Parliament relies, faced the dilemma of a member who actively opposed the policy of the party leader. The association voted on a motion of censure on their MP, which they rejected by a majority of only three to two. One vote the other way, and Churchill would have been expected to resign his seat and stand again for re-election. It is doubtful whether he could have recovered his popularity against the pressure of the official party machine, and difficult to see how he could have re-established a place in politics before the opening of hostilities. Britain would ultimately have been forced to adopt an alternative leader, and history might have followed a very different course.

So Churchill remained a member of parliament, and his country moved steadily towards war with Germany. The Germans failed to honour the. Munich agreement, occupied the whole of Czechoslovakia, and turned their attention towards Poland. As a result of these events major changes occurred in the British political scene. Chamberlain, although still anxious to preserve peace, recognised that Hitler had betrayed the trust which

he had placed in him, and that their agreement would not be honoured. On 17th March in a speech in Birmingham he completely reversed his policy of conciliation; he deplored Hitler's failure to keep to the terms of the Munich agreement, and expressed his disappointment and indignation that their hopes for Hitler's declaration of no further territorial claims after the occupation of the Sudetenland had been shattered. Two weeks later, his faith in Hitler's reliability destroyed, and inspired by a new determination to protect other small European states from Hitler's depredations, Chamberlain declared his country's assurance that they would come to the aid of Poland if that nation's independence were threatened, and that France had declared likewise.

No doubt Hitler placed great reliance on the likelihood of further vacillation from Britain, but if he did so he seriously misread the changing mood of the British government and the British people. Having tried the course of appeasement for so long, and seen it fail, Britain was only too ready to resort to the only other honourable course and from the moment of the declaration on Poland it became inevitable that if Hitler continued to pursue his current activities in Europe, war between the two countries would take place. At the same time if followed that Winston Churchill's prospects of becoming a member of the government approached nearer to certainty. There was a considerable upsurge in public opinion and in the press in favour of the formation of a National Government comprised of members of all the major parties, and including Churchill, but his inclusion would in Chamberlain's view be open to interpretation by Hitler as an unnecessarily hostile gesture, and Churchill therefore remained outside the government throughout the spring and summer months of 1939.

During this time he continued his commentary on the European scene, and concerned himself most especially with the pact which was formed between Hitler and the Soviet Union, out of which ultimately flowed the invasion of Poland. On 16th April the Soviet government formally proposed the creation of a united front between Britain, France, and themselves, which would guarantee the security of those eastern and central European powers which faced German aggression. At approximately the same time however the Russian government began through its ambassador in Berlin to explore the possibility of improving relations between their two countries.

During the next few weeks the British government made no direct response to the Soviet overture, and on 4th May Churchill pleaded that no further time should be lost, claiming that for the safety of the Baltic states a friendly Russia supplying munitions and other aid was essential: 'There is no means of maintaining an Eastern front against Nazi aggression without the active aid of Russia . . . It should still be possible to range all the States and people from the Baltic to the Black Sea in one solid front against a new outrage or invasion. Such a front, if established in good heart, and with resolute and efficient military arrangements, combined with the strength of the Western Powers, may yet confront Hitler, Göring, Himmler, Ribbentrop, Goebbels and Co with forces the German people would be reluctant to challenge.'

But the British government still failed to achieve an agreement. A series of exchanges went on through the diplomatic machinery, in which the British government tried to induce the Soviet government to make declarations with them of mutual cooperation and assistance, but without a full-hearted formal pact. Based on such niceties of diplomacy, this elaborate manoeuvring was almost certain to fail, and Churchill made clear his objections to it. On 19th May the House of Commons debated the

matter, and Churchill again, with a plainness of outlook which was to become familiar, pleaded at length for acceptance of the Russian overture: 'I have been quite unable to understand what is the objection to making the agreement with Russia which the Prime Minister professes himself desirous of doing, and making it in the broad and simple form proposed by the Russian Soviet government . . . The alliance is solely for the purpose of resisting further acts of aggression and of protecting the victims of aggression. I cannot see what is wrong with that. What is wrong with this simple proposal?'

Later he spoke at length about the guarantee to Poland and the necessity of an eastern front: 'It is a tremendous thing, this question of an Eastern front. I am astonished that there is not more anxiety about it. Certainly I do not ask favours of Soviet Russia. This is no time to ask favours of countries. But here is an offer, a fair offer, and a better offer, in my opinion, than the terms which the Government seek to get for themselves; a more simple, a more direct and a more effective offer. Let it not be put aside and come to nothing. I beg His Majesty's Government to get some of these brutal truths into their heads. Without an effective Eastern front there can be no satisfactory defence of our interests in the West, and without Russia there can be no effective Eastern front.'

By this time, however, Russia's relations with Germany were maturing and making such appeals irrelevant. Both Germany and Russia reversed their former policies and attempted to work together, and while the British made a half-hearted attempt during June and July to re-establish negotiations with the Soviet Union, the governments of Hitler and Stalin made positive progress. On 23rd August they signed a non-aggression pact which included arrangements for the partition of Poland, and Britain's potentially valuable links with the

The expansion of Nazi Germany

**Stalin and Ribbentrop seal the
Russo-German non-aggression pact**

Soviet Union were lost.

The British Prime Minister, in a letter to Hitler, affirmed that the Soviet-German pact would in no way alter Great Britain's obligation to Poland, which His Majesty's government were determined to fulfil. At the same time the government proceeded to underline their somehwat forlorn intentions of protecting the small state of Poland from the wealthy, powerful, and numerous forces ranged against it by taking a number of minor mobilisation measures. They called out the key men to operate anti-aircraft defences, ordered the conversion of thirty-five merchantmen into armed merchant cruisers, arranged for thirty trawlers to be fitted with sonar devices as submarine hunters, called up thirty thousand reservists, and stopped all leave among the services.

On 25th August they also drew up a formal agreement ratifying their guarantee to Poland, and waited for Hitler to move. In fact Hitler postponed his proposed D-Day from 25th August until 1st September, and on the last day of August issued his 'Directive Number 1 for the Conduct of the War'. It stated: 'Now that all the political possibilities of disposing by peaceful means of a situation on the Eastern frontier which is intolerable for Germany are exhausted, I have determined on a solution by force.' The attack on Poland was to begin at 0445 on 1st September.

Winston Churchill, at home at Chartwell, knew full well that as soon as hostilities began he would be a prominent target for the thousands of Nazi sympathisers who operated in England. As a private member of Parliament he enjoyed no official protection, but with exemplary foresight he quickly produced his own solution to the problem. He contacted his old bodyguard from his days in government, a retired Scot-

Above : Germany's expansion continues : the Wehrmacht drives into Poland.
Below : Britain declares war. The crowd in Downing Street hurry away after the announcement on the morning of 3rd September 1939

Mr Churchill with his humble duty to Your Majesty
has the honour to submit the accompanying photographs
of the new 15" howitzer.

Twelve of these guns are under construction. The first
two are ready, and will be shipped to France this week,
where it is proposed that they should come into action
next Thursday. Two more will follow at the end of
the month, and the remainder at regular intervals.
There is sufficient ammunition for the early firings,
and increasing quantities will be steadily forthcoming.

The building of these guns, from the designs and under
the supervision of Rear Admiral Bacon, constitutes
a record in production, having been entirely carried
out since the war began.
The proof firings exceeded in excellence all previous
estimates — 11,000 yards being attained instead of 10,000.
Winston S. Churchill

Churchill reports to the King on the new guns, 1915. He raised the subject again on his return to the Admiralty in 1939

land Yard detective called Inspector Thomson, and called him down to Chartwell. Together they resurrected their long unused pistols, checked them over, and then took it in turns to sleep and watch. 'Nobody', Churchill wrote in his memoirs, 'would have had a walk-over.'

On the morning of 1st September Germany duly attacked Poland, and during that afternoon Chamberlain called Churchill to see him. He indicated that he now saw no possibility of avoiding war, and invited Churchill to join a small war cabinet which he was to form. Churchill accepted.

Strangely enough, Chamberlain still appears to have tried to retain total personal control over foreign policy. He failed to inform Churchill that the government of which he was now an important member was on the point of issuing the first of two ultimatums to Hitler. Churchill in fact remained entirely out of touch throughout the second day of September, despite a plaintive appeal by letter to Chamberlain to put him in the picture, and was not told that a second ultimatum had been issued and rejected on the morning of 3rd September. It was only when Chamberlain broadcast to the nation by radio, at 11.45 on the morning of 3rd September, that Churchill learned, at the same time as millions of other citizens, that his country had already declared war on Germany.

Almost immediately after this broadcast, the wailing of the air-raid warning sirens, a noise which was to become so familiar to the British people during the next five years, sounded over London for the first time, and Churchill went with his wife on to their flat roof, where they saw the barrage of anti-aircraft balloons slowly rise around the city. After some minutes of watching, Churchill and his wife went down to their air-raid shelter in a nearby basement, and passed some ten minutes in the good-natured company of their neighbours, while Churchill contemplated the terrible destruction and loss of life which he expected such raids to bring. About ten minutes later the all-clear signal sounded; it appeared that the intruding enemy had been a small private aircraft arriving unannounced from France, and Churchill and his fellow Londoners went about their business unharmed. Churchill crossed to the House of Commons, where, he records in his memoirs, he felt a very strong sense of calm come over him: 'I felt a serenity of mind and was conscious of a kind of uplifted detachment from human and personal affairs. The glory of Old England, peace-loving and ill-prepared as she was, but instant and fearless at the call of honour, thrilled my being and seemed to lift our fate to those spheres far removed from earthly facts and physical sensation.'

That afternoon, Chamberlain began to emerge from the mysterious silence of the preceding few days, and invited Churchill to see him in his room at the House. There he offered Churchill the post of First Lord of the Admiralty, which would now, with the other two service ministries, be a post within the war cabinet. Churchill was delighted. The greatest and happiest days of his life had been spent as First Lord during the First World War, before he was removed from the post in the political upheavals which followed the abortive Dardanelles campaign. Now he wasted no time in returning there. Although his appointment was not to be formally confirmed until two days later he sent word to the Admiralty that he was on his way, and at six o'clock that evening arrived at the room which, he wrote, 'I had quitted in pain and sorrow almost exactly a quarter of a century before . . .' There he found the same chair he had used, the map case he had fixed to the wall behind it; even his favourite octagonal table was resurrected from a store room.

The Admiralty were clearly as pleased to have Churchill back as he was glad to be there, for they promptly signalled to the entire fleet the simple affectionate message: 'Winston is back'.

Whether it was in the nature of the war itself, or whether Churchill had a natural knack of finding himself at the centre of things, the Admiralty from the moment of his arrival became the focal point of Britain's war effort. For the British army and the Royal Air Force, the war brought little marked change, and indeed settled into an autumn and winter of curious peacefulness. But at sea nothing was peaceful. Three hours after Churchill's arrival at the Admiralty a U-boat in the Atlantic torpedoed and sank the passenger liner *Athenia*, and 112 people were drowned. Churchill

immediately became a figure of attention when German propaganda officials circulated a claim that he had ordered the ship to be sabotaged to discredit Germany and destroy her relations with the United States, a number of whose citizens were among those lost.

After this devastating introduction, Churchill applied himself to the problems of his new post with an energy and devotion which few had anticipated and which many at first found unwelcome and inconvenient. He spent most of that first night meeting the Sea Lords, the senior admirals who were to work alongside him, and talking to the department heads, and soon he was familiar with the situation at sea. At ten o'clock the following morning he was back at work, and almost immediately drafted the first of innumerable minutes which were to form his main line of communication in office in the Second World War. This first message set a pattern for the future with its terseness, its clarity,

Churchill after his return to government following his resignation after the Dardanelles operation. He is pictured as Secretary of State for War in 1918. Upheavals and controversy were features of his long political career

and the searching nature of its contents: 'Let me have a statement of the German U-boat forces, actual and prospective, for the next few months. Please distinguish between ocean-going and small-size U-Boats. Give the estimated radius of action in days and miles in each case.'

Later that night he held his first Admiralty conference, and at the end of it, far from falling into bed for an exhausted sleep to recover from the fatigue of the preceding thirty-six hours, he stayed up and dictated for circulation a lengthy account of the conclusions of the meeting. At ten o'clock the next morning he was in conference once again, this time settling the question of a safe base for the home fleet.

Having familiarised himself with the situation at the Admiralty, Churchill had no hesitation in in-

U-Boat, the object of Churchill's concern in his first minute as the new First Lord

volving himself in the affairs of other ministries. On 10th September he wrote to the Prime Minister a long letter on questions far outside the scope of his own department, but on which he felt his experience and knowledge entitled him to make a meaningful comment. They included the institution of bombing raids by the Royal Air Force on civilian targets (the RAF, he said, should not take the initiative), the shortage of heavy artillery among the British Expedit-

ionary Force, the naval construction programme, and the supply problems of the air force and the army. He also wrote that day to the Minister of Supply suggesting that he should recover and recondition the store of artillery which Churchill had laid down when at the War Office in 1919; the Minister wrote back in the kindest terms that they had been devoting themselves to exactly that project for the past year.

Churchill's stream of letters continued, ranging over the whole field,

and including an extraordinary one to
the Chancellor of the Exchequer recommending all possible economies:
'Take stationery, for example – this
should be regulated at once in all
departments. Envelopes should be
pasted up and re-directed again and
again. Although this seems a small
thing, it teaches every official – and
we now have millions of them – to
think of saving.'

This remarkable burst of activity
indicated several facets of Churchill's
character and attitudes at this time.
Clearly he did not regard himself as
bound by the limitations of his office
to naval questions only. On the contrary he felt it was his business to
poke around in any area where he
felt he could make a contribution.
Not that he was insensitive to the
prospect of becoming thoroughly un-
popular through interfering in other
people's work. Indeed he took steps
to disarm his colleagues from making
that accusation: 'I hope you will not
mind me writing to you upon this
subject'. It was rather, at this stage
at least, that he felt such sensitivity
must be subordinated to the simple,
straightforward, and uncomplicated
aim of winning the war. Perhaps
partly for that reason, perhaps partly
because he already saw himself as the
overall war leader in the near future,
Churchill was also willing to subordinate the interests of his own
department to those of the combined
war effort. As he wrote to Chamberlain: 'There are great dangers in
giving absolute priority to any department. In the late war the Admiralty used their priority arbitrarily
and selfishly, especially in the last
year, when they were overwhelmingly
strong, and had the American Navy
added to them. I am every day re-
straining such tendencies in the
common interest.'

While he was establishing the pattern for his own methods of communication with his colleagues and
associates, Churchill was in several
other respects setting precedents and
laying foundations for his methods of
working. One was his insistence on
getting out and about the country,
despite the massive burden of desk-
work which his office involved. On
14th September he set out on a visit
to Scapa Flow, where the Home
Fleet was stationed. He felt it was his
duty to meet the Admiral in command and his officers and seamen,
and he clearly relished the opportunity to get away from the con-
fined atmosphere of London and see
for himself what was happening. He
continued to travel tirelessly throughout the war, and by doing so not only
kept in constant touch with the
affairs which it was his job to control,
but exerted a marked effect on the
morale of the men fighting the war.

Shortly before he left on this visit,
Churchill set another precedent. On
11th September President Roosevelt
wrote to him expressing pleasure at
Churchill's return to the Admiralty:
'What I want you and the Prime
Minister to know is that I shall at all
times welcome it if you will keep me
in touch personally with anything
you want me to know about.' The
letter gave Churchill an enormous
lift. He replied at once, signed himself
'Naval Person' and by that early
exchange of letters struck up a relationship which was to prove not
only one of the most personally
rewarding of his life, but also a vital
element in the prosecution of the war.

Then on 1st October he made his
first radio broadcast since taking
office, in which he dealt with the
problem of Russia: 'I cannot forecast
to you the action of Russia,' he said.
'It is a riddle wrapped in a mystery
inside an enigma. But perhaps there is
a key. That key is Russian national
interest.' By that broadcast he showed
that he was prepared to use the
medium of radio to keep the British

The *Admiral Graf von Spee*, scuttled and burning off the River Plate

people fully informed on the course of the war. In all these areas he laid foundations during those first three weeks on which he was to build heavily during the course of the war.

At the end of his visit to Scapa Flow, Churchill travelled by overnight train to London, and was greeted at Euston station by his First Sea Lord, Admiral Sir Dudley Pound, who looked grave. Pound had come personally to give him the news that the aircraft carrier *Courageous* had been sunk on the previous evening in the Bristol Channel. Churchill replied: 'We can't expect to carry on a war like this without that sort of thing happening from time to time. I have seen lots of it before.'

At the end of the month he was able to redress the balance somewhat by telling the House of Commons that the figures for merchant shipping being sunk by the U-Boats was falling dramatically, from 64,000 tons in the first week to fewer than 5,000 tons in the last week of the month. Only a fortnight later, however, the picture changed again when a U-Boat commanded by Lieutenant Gunther Prien penetrated the defences of Scapa Flow, which Churchill had so recently inspected, and sank the battleship *Royal Oak* with torpedoes. 786 men were killed. This heavy loss, and the incursion into the supposedly safe anchorage in homely Scotland, deeply shocked the British nation and, as Churchill acknowledged, might in normal circumstances have led to the political downfall of the minister responsible. But Churchill as a newly appointed First Lord was not held responsible for the incident and survived.

He was able to report better news after 19th December. On that day ended the first major naval engagement of the war, when the Royal Navy finally tracked down and engaged the pocket battleship *Admiral Graf von*

Spee, which had been operating successfully for several months as a surface raider mainly in the southern Atlantic. Three cruisers, *Ajax*, *Achilles* and *Exeter*, fought a brief but fierce battle with the *Graf von Spee* and forced her to flee to shelter in the neutral harbour at Montevideo, while they waited offshore for her reappearance. At the end of the time the ship was permitted to remain in port, her commander transferred most of his men to a merchant ship, sailed out to sea, and scuttled her, before finally committing suicide. The incident restored Britain's naval prestige and confidence to an enormous extent, and was followed in mid-February by a further heartening incident, in which British destroyers intercepted the *Graf von Spee*'s auxiliary, the *Altmark*, which was suspected of carrying British prisoners taken off ships which the *Graf von Spee* had sunk. Despite assurances that Nor-

wegian officers had searched the ship and found her empty, Churchill personally ordered the destroyer *Cossack* to close, and its commander Captain Philip Vian to search the ship. Vian assembled a boarding party, grappled the *Altmark*, and after a short hand-to-hand fight opened the hatches and discovered 299 British prisoners. Somebody shouted 'The Navy's here' and that cry subsequently entered, alongside Nelson's signal before Trafalgar, the annals of British naval tradition.

Not for the first time, Churchill had taken a great personal gamble. Had the Norwegians been right and no prisoners been on board, he would have provoked an international

The *Altmark, Graf von Spee*'s auxiliary, discovered in Josing Fjord. Nearly 300 British prisoners were found aboard when she was subsequently captured by *HMS Cossack*

incident. But the risk proved justified, and the surge of faith in the navy's strength and determination which followed these events restored the prestige of the Admiralty and greatly improved Churchill's personal position.

These incidents however were merely minor events in the course of Churchill's career. The issue which most deeply affected his future during this period was a larger campaign, the British involvement in Norway, and indeed it came close to bringing about his downfall, until by an ironic combination of circumstances it in fact turned the course of his career in the opposite, and entirely successful, direction.

Churchill had long been fascinated by the strategic importance of Norway, as indeed had Hitler, who later called it the 'zone of destiny'. His new concern began when he tried to revive a plan formed during the First World War to block the Leads, the Norwegian territorial waters which German merchant shipping used during winter when the Gulf of Bosnia froze. Mining the Leads would block the traffic in Swedish iron ore, on which Germany's industry relied, by forcing the ships out on to the high seas where they could be arrested for carrying contraband or captured as prizes. On 16th December Churchill put before the cabinet a long and detailed paper in which he outlined the strategic benefits of such a step,

explored the implications, and foresaw the dangers. He visualised that the Germans could well respond by invading Norway and Sweden, but thought that the British, backed by superior power at sea, could throw them out of all the important points along the coast and could maintain an absolute blockade. He also drew attention to the need to suspend the stricter dictates of conscience in order to achieve the reign of law and protect the liberties of small countries: 'Our defeat would mean an age of barbaric violence, and would be fatal not only to ourselves, but to the independent life of every small country in Europe . . . Small nations must not tie our hands when we are fighting

The Germans move into Norway, and the phoney war comes to an end

for their rights and freedom.'

It happened that about this time Hitler had in fact arrived at his decision to invade Norway, and in February he expounded to one of his generals the basis of his thinking: 'The occupation of Norway by the British would be a strategic turning movement which would lead them into the Baltic, where we have neither troops nor coastal fortifications . . . the enemy would find himself in a position to advance on Berlin . . . the conquest of Norway (by Germany) will ensure the liberty of movement of our Fleet in the Bay of Wilhelmshaven,

A British success at Narvik ; a German destroyer lies scuttled in Rombaks Fjord

and will protect our imports of Swedish ore.'

Hitler's exposition, reported by Falkenhorst at the Nuremberg trials, showed exactly how accurate Churchill's thinking had been.

On 16th March Hitler, on the recommendation of Admiral Raeder, fixed the date of his invasion of Norway provisionally for 9th April. On 3rd April the British cabinet, seven months after Churchill had first raised the issue, authorised the mining of the Leads, to take place on 8th April. Thus the two antagonists moved independently towards action in Norway. Neither side could blame the other for having precipitated the conflict, and Norway stood a victim of its own strategic importance. When the conflict did arrive, it turned out to be a military success for Hitler, a disgraceful failure for the British.

Hitler's devastating assault, using airborne troops to their greatest effect, took place on 9th April, and in London the War Cabinet authorised Churchill to order the Home Fleet to clear Bergen and Trondheim of enemy forces and mount a military operation to capture those ports and occupy Narvik. Initially at Narvik the Royal Navy acquitted itself well, until they were badly mauled by the arrival of German destroyer reinforcements. Narvik remained in German hands, and Churchill confessed that the British had been forestalled, surprised, and outwitted. It became obvious that the capture of Narvik would entail a long and costly fight. The House of Commons, like the country, was angry, and Churchill had to defend the record in the debate on 11th April. He won the sympathy of the House by his frank account of events, while blaming the neutral countries themselves for holding the Allies at arms length until actually attacked. His reputation survived, but there was more to follow.

After a second naval operation on 13th April it was decided to send an expedition to land at Harstad and subsequently take Narvik. The orders to the army commander were indecisive, he was made to share the command decision with the naval commander, and the expedition in any case was badly equipped. Despite pressure from the naval commander Lord Cork, the army commander General Mackesey refused to go ahead with the assault, and no amount of pressure from London could make him do so. He preferred to wait around for the snows to melt.

As this fiasco developed, a second operation was being planned against the equally important port of Trondheim to the south. The planning staffs in London agreed on a bold, imaginative, and ambitious plan for a frontal assault from the sea, but changed their minds in view of the air risk to ships, and opted for a land assault from both sides of Trondheim, where at Mamsos and Andalsnes small British forces already had a toehold. Both these assaults failed to make worthwhile progress, and the troops were evacuated.

At Narvik the assault was held up through inertia and lack of co-ordinated planning until mid-May, but by then events in France made it obvious that all troops engaged in Norway would have to be withdrawn for service elsewhere. The port was ultimately captured with little German resistance and hardly any loss on 28th May, the troops were taken off, and the entire Norwegian adventure was abandoned.

A crucial debate on the progress of the Norwegian operation began on 7th May, and from the start both Chamberlain and the government in general were fiercely attacked for their conduct. Admiral of the Fleet Sir Roger Keyes, the heroic leader of the raid on Zeebrugge during the First World War and now a Conservative member of parliament, rose wearing admiral's full dress uniform. He spoke with great authority and severely attacked the government for

Admiral of the Fleet Sir Roger Keyes

its lack of boldness in failing to capture Trondheim. Another leading and respected Conservative, Leo Amery, reiterated the words in which Oliver Cromwell had three hundred years earlier berated the Long Parliament: 'You have sat too long here for any good you have been doing. Depart, I say, and let us have done with you. In the name of God, go!' Then Lloyd George, in his last major Parliamentary speech, called for Chamberlain's resignation: '. . . the Prime Minister should give an example of sacrifice, because there is nothing which can contribute more to victory in this war than that he should sacrifice the seals of office.'

Churchill, winding up the debate, attempted to defend the Prime Minister, but the weight of opinion against him was overwhelming. It had been one of the most dramatic debates of modern times, and at the end of it the government achieved

The panzers assemble for Hitler's
invasion of France

a majority of only 81, a savage reduction of their normal majority of some 240. Herbert Morrison had described the debate as a vote of confidence in the Prime Minister, and in effect, if not in numbers, Chamberlain had lost that vote. After the debate he called Churchill to see him, and in a deeply depressed state said that he felt a national government was the only answer and that he was prepared to stand down in favour of another leader who could command the support of all parties.

For the next two days the situation remained fluid and uncertain, until on the afternoon of 9th May the Prime Minister called together at 10 Downing Street the three most important figures in the parliamentary hierarchy: Churchill, Lord Halifax, and the government chief whip. Chamberlain again said that he had made up his mind to resign, and that his successor must be either Halifax or Churchill. Halifax

agreed that the Prime Minister should go, but thought that it would be impossible for him to take on the job: as a member of the House of Lords he would not be permitted to enter the House of Commons, and he would be responsible for the conduct of the war but unable to influence the body on whose confidence the life of the government would depend. Chamberlain was evidently in favour of Lord Halifax taking over his office, but he reluctantly accepted Halifax's view. It therefore became clear that the task would fall on Churchill.

On the morning of the next day, 10th May, German forces began their invasion of Belgium, Holland, and Luxemburg. London was alive with news of the invasion and for a time the cabinet crisis faded into the background. Indeed at a cabinet meeting that day Chamberlain said that he felt compelled by this momentous news to remain Prime Minister, but the Labour leaders let it be known that they would not take part in a national government under him. Late that afternoon Chamberlain, having hung on for so long, finally went to Buckingham Palace to tender his resignation to King George VI. Under the British constitution it is technically the King who appoints the Prime Minister, and invites him to form a government, although the monarch invariably discusses the appointment with the outgoing First Minister. On this occasion King George VI suggested Halifax, who he thought was 'the obvious man'. Chamberlain however explained the obstacle, and recommended Churchill.

Of all the countries in the world it is probable that only Great Britain, at war for eight months and facing the real peril of German armed aggression in nearby countries, could allow the one man favoured by both the Prime Minister and the King to be barred from leading the nation by the circumstances of his birth. The King in fact would have been happy to set aside Halifax's peerage and let him

King George VI and his Prime Minister, Mr Churchill

do the job. But no, a commoner it had to be, and there was only one choice. Ironically Churchill also was a member of an old aristocratic family, was in fact the grandson of a duke, and was only by a bare margin spared the inconvenience of being born to a peerage. Whether Halifax would have made a better Prime Minister than Churchill is impossible to judge, but Churchill it was whom the British nation were to get as leader, and at six o'clock that night he was called to the palace. The King, indulging himself for a few moments in an innocent private joke said: 'I suppose you don't know why I have sent for you?' Churchill played him along briefly: 'Sir, I simply couldn't imagine why.' And then the King laughed and told him: 'I want to ask you to form a government.'

There is no doubt that Churchill approached the prospect with great relish. He enjoyed being in charge, and would enjoy conducting the war in his own way. That night he started appointing the key figures in his cabinet, and ended a long and eventful day in the small hours: '... as I went to bed at about 3 am I was conscious of a profound sense of relief. At last I had the authority to give directions over the whole scene. I felt as if I were walking with destiny, and that all my past life had been but a preparation for this hour and for this trial. Ten years in the political wilderness had freed me from ordinary party antagonisms. My warnings over the last six years had been so numerous, so detailed, and were now so terribly vindicated, that no one could gainsay me. I could not be reproached either for making the war or with want of preparation for it. I thought I knew a good deal about it all, and I was sure I should not fail. Therefore, although impatient for the morning, I slept soundly and had no need for cheering dreams. Facts are better than dreams.'

The Summer of 1940

Churchill's accession to the premiership was by no means universally acclaimed. British taste in political leaders strongly favours the colourless, the predictable, the unexciting, and Churchill was none of these. He was known to be highly emotional in temperament and thought to be unstable in judgement, and his political record, particularly during the First World War, indicated that he was prone to take large-scale risks, sometimes in defiance of orthodox military theory. The widely held view was that he was brilliant but unreliable.

Such misgivings were widespread among those who in May 1940 knew

that they would have to work with him, the civil servants and military advisers who formed the complex permanent or semi-permanent machinery of government. There was a feeling throughout Whitehall that he was too much an individual to become the successful leader of a team, that he was meddlesome and inclined to interfere in departments which were none of his concern, that he was verbose, and that this combination of qualities was certain to lead to friction and difficulties in planning.

Even King George VI had difficulty in accepting that Churchill had become his First Minister. On the morning after appointing Churchill he met Halifax walking through the garden of Buckingham Palace (a privilege enjoyed by the few who can obtain special permission) and told him, in what might now no doubt be considered a major royal indiscretion, that he was sorry not to have him as Prime Minister.

But all this was soon to change; not only for the King and for Churchill's political and administrative colleagues, but also for the British people.

For the administration, the change in attitudes came as soon as they

Home Guard volunteers begin basic training

began to see the pace at which Churchill worked and the methods he used. Within a short time all the people around him found that the tempo of their lives had suddenly increased by a remarkable margin. Work which had proceeded at its normal leisurely pace throught the months of the phoney war was quite abruptly transformed. The flow of minutes which Churchill had begun on his arrival at the Admiralty increased, and now that he had the authority to back his impulsive curiosity they began to pour into every corner of the nation's business. Men who had worked quietly in their own departments for months or years suddenly found themselves addressed with a personal memorandum from the Prime Minister. All of these minutes were worded in such a way as to demand action, and the Prime Minister's messages injected a new sense of urgency into the lives of the civil servants and planning staffs. If the matter was one of extreme urgency, Churchill clipped to the minute a vivid red label bearing the words ACTION THIS DAY, which

Chequers

effectively removed all chance of procrastination. Nor did he devote himself, even in these days of European disaster, solely to questions of international importance: his attention to detail was profound, and he wrote memoranda on matters as divorced from the normally expected range of the Prime Minister's interests as whether the troops could be issued with wax to protect their ears during combat, and what arrangements had been made to look after the animals in the London zoo in the event of a bombardment.

Ordinary working hours were abandoned, as were any distinctions between office and home, leisure and work. Churchill worked at all hours, and in any place. Secretaries and staff would find themselves taking dictation or bringing papers to Churchill in his bedroom, and a secretary often travelled with him in his car. There, if he were not taking advantage of the journey to sleep, he made use of every available moment to go through his papers and dictate minutes or speeches: he apparently found the motion of the car conducive to clear thought and effective composition.

After the first few hectic days of his premiership, his life settled into something resembling a routine. He generally woke at about eight o'clock and called immediately for his 'box' – the cabinet box in which his work was assembled. He worked through its contents, generally staying in bed

until about mid-day, at which time, though seldom earlier, he began the day's meetings. After lunch, which like other main meals was used for discussion about the war, he would sleep for an hour. Churchill regarded his ability to sleep during the day as a precious gift, and did not devalue it by taking light naps: when not travelling, he always undressed and went to bed for a deep and refreshing sleep which had the effect, he said, of enabling him to fit a day-and-a-half's work into each twenty-four hours. 'Nature had not intended mankind to work from eight in the morning until mid-night without that refreshment of blessed oblivion which, even if it only lasts twenty minutes, is sufficient to renew all the vital forces. This routine I observed throughout the war, and I commend it to others if and when they find it necessary for a long spell to get the last scrap out of the human structure.' After his siesta he would take a bath and emerge ready to begin again, holding more meetings, giving more dictation, until dinner, which he again used for meeting and discussions. After dinner work would start yet again. Either he returned to his box, working through its contents and dictating minutes, or he would keep his colleagues up for interminable conversation. He had no compunction about calling in even the most senior officials and military chiefs even if it were long past midnight. It was not that he was callous in his demands: according to those who knew him well, it simply never occured to him that other people might observe a routine different from his own. This last phase of the day's work went on until two or perhaps three in the morning, at which time he would finally go to bed, and without the slightest delay fall into a deep sleep from which he would wake totally refreshed at about eight the following morning.

Weekends brought no change in the routine, except that he normally moved with his entourage to Chequers,

the official country residence of British Prime Ministers in Buckinghamshire. There the flow of minutes would be maintained, and the only departure from the practice observed at 10 Downing Street was the larger number of visitors, consisting of an international cast list of statesmen, politicians and service chiefs. There meal-times were again used exclusively for talking over the business of running the war. Although Churchill abhorred small-talk, conversation was his one major outlet during the war, but it always centred on the problems of the day, and since Churchill was not the greatest of listeners, it often degenerated into a monologue. His other main form of relaxation during the war was a private showing of a film, which took place almost every night when he was at Chequers, and the entire party was expected to join him to watch it. Often their enjoyment would be less than full-hearted, for they quickly learned that after the film they would often be called on to start work again, sacrificing all hopes of an early night.

Churchill has often been criticised for his methods of working. He was indeed no great administrator, and had little respect for formalities of organisation. He often cut through protocol and made contact with people whom his staff thought he was wrong to be spending time with, yet it was only his natural curiosity which made him keen to find out his facts at first hand, and long experience had made him fear that organisations were liable to conceal information from him. He was often accused of meddling in trifling affairs, of devoting his attention to questions at an excessively detailed level, even as far down as the correct pronunciation of foreign place names. No doubt many of these criticisms were justified, but the people who in the initial stages of their dealings with Churchill found that his methods led to friction and inconvenience, soon learned to accommodate or ignore the difficulties and concentrate on the benefits. When they found they were dealing with a man whose energy, drive, and forcefulness were arousing in a torpid nation a new determination to fight for its life, they quickly learned to accept his foibles and eccentric behaviour.

Churchill's methods of working provided adequate compensation for his faults. Despite his addiction to conversation, he kept verbal contact with his subordinates to a minimum and left people to get on with their jobs without interference. It was his practice to communicate with them almost exclusively in writing, and during the summer of 1940 he issued a directive on the subject. He claims in his memoirs that the intention was to 'make sure that his name was not used loosely', but in addition the practice served to crystallise his own thoughts, and to give clear and unambiguous directions to the addressee: 'Let it be very clearly understood that all directions emanating from me are made in writing, or should be immediately afterwards confirmed in writing, and that I do not accept any responsibility for matters relating to national defence on which I am alleged to have given directions unless they are recorded in writing.'

This method was a discipline to Churchill. He was by profession a journalist and author, as much as a politician, and he was at his best when communicating in writing, both in minutes and in his speeches, which were in fact formally worded essays read without departure from the text. He had his own highly individual technique for composition, in which he dictated almost everything he wrote. Not that his dictation was especially fast or easy: it was indeed a long and sometimes arduous process. He employed several secretaries, including a male shorthand writer who accompanied him on long journeys abroad, and he preferred to work with staff whose faces were familiar to him. He expected them, like everybody else,

to be masters of their jobs, and made no concessions to them either in the conditions in which they worked or in terms of his uncertain audibility. In a state of intense concentration he would pace up and down a room, rolling phrases around his lips, and waving his hands in impressive gestures, until he had decided on exactly the correct word or phrase which he then delivered to the secretary, who worked either in shorthand or directly on to a typewriter. Long practice had enabled him to perfect this art, and once he had committed himself he seldom changed what he had written.

His way of life and methods of working were no doubt extremely odd, but the indisputable fact was that for him they worked. He knew exactly how he functioned best, and he did so with supreme effectiveness. Churchill was obviously an extremely demanding man to work for. He could be fierce and ill-tempered, but never for more than a moment: he could be totally insensitive to people, but was deeply sorry if he found that he had hurt anyone through negligence; he pretended that he was ruthless, and in fact could sack without the slightest hestitation if he felt a change of personnel would be an improvement, yet he had enormous sympathy with people who suffered through no fault of their own. He was in fact a man of great contradictions, and although he was in some respects a most unlikeable person, within a short time of his arrival in the premiership everybody around him developed an admiration for him which amounted to adoration, and of all those who recorded their thoughts on the subject after the war, none gave any hint of a serious or lasting dislike.

And just as he abruptly transformed the attitudes of his various staffs, Churchill quickly worked the same magic both on his political colleagues and on the British people. He did so by means of a remarkable series of speeches, most of them delivered initially in parliament and repeated

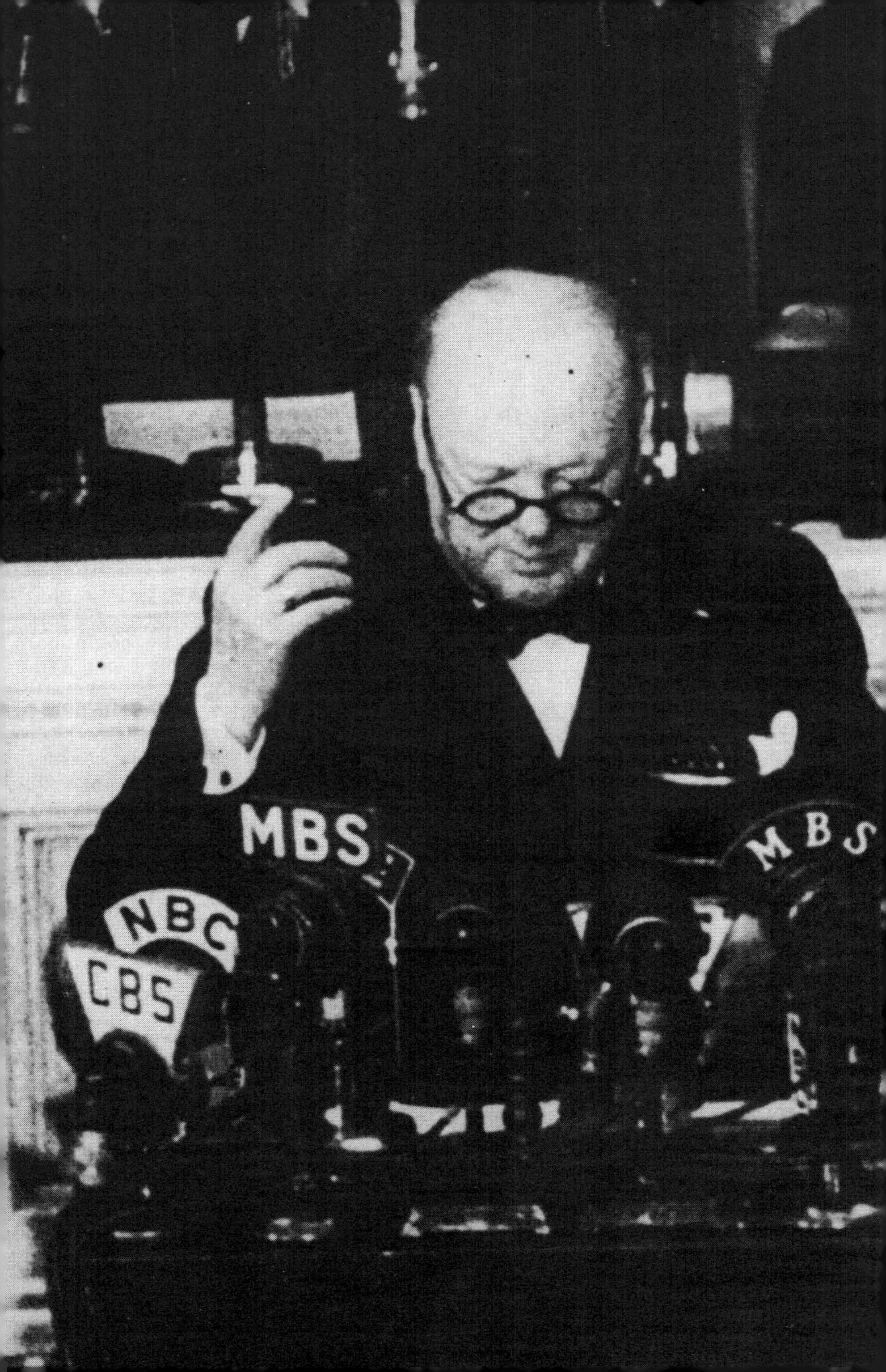
MBS
NBC
CBS
MBS

Left : The orator. *Above :* General Gamelin and Lord Gort at a conference with Churchill before the French debacle. *Right :* Paul Reynaud, Premier of France

immediately afterwards as radio broadcasts.

The course of the war during that summer of 1940 could hardly have gone more severely against the British people, short of a successful invasion of the British Isles by Hitler's armies. Churchill realistically foresaw this period of adversity and in his first speech to the House of Commons as Prime Minister, during a special sitting on 13th May aimed at securing a vote of confidence in the new government, he soberly presented the prospects to his colleagues: 'I would say to the House, as I said to those who have joined this government: I have nothing to offer but blood, toil, tears, and sweat . . . You ask, What is our policy? I will say: it is to wage war by sea, land, and air, with all our might and with all the strength that God can give us; to wage war against a monstrous tyranny, never surpassed in the dark, lamentable catalogue of human crime. That is our policy. You ask, what is our aim? I can answer in one word. It is victory, victory at all costs, victory in spite of all terror, victory however long and hard the road may be – for without victory there is no survival. Let that be realized – no survival for the British Empire, no survival for all the British Empire has stood for, no survival for the urge and impulse of the ages, that mankind will move forward towards its goal. But I take up my task with buoyancy and hope. I feel sure that our cause will not be suffered to fail among men. At this time I feel entitled to claim the aid of all, and I say, "Come, then, let us go forward together with our united strength".'

The House gave Churchill a unanimous vote of confidence, then adjourned for a week, during which time Churchill was confronted with a most staggering succession of setbacks.

On the morning of 14th May news began to come in of the impending German breakthrough at Sedan. On the morning of 15th May the Dutch army surrendered, and the pressure

on the French line was such that the French high command virtually gave up hope. The Premier, M Reynaud, telephoned Churchill in bed and told him in English: 'We are beaten. We have lost the battle.' Churchill could not believe that it had happened so soon, but Reynaud went on: 'The front is broken near Sedan.'

The situation deteriorated throughout that day as the French army and the British Expeditionary Force withdrew, and the following afternoon Churchill flew to Paris to see what he could do. There he found the French high command in the depths of despair. They had collected in a room at the Quai D'Orsay and were spending their time wandering around in small disconsolate groups discussing the situation. On Churchill's arrival they assembled in front of an easel, and with the aid of a map General Gamelin, the Commander-in-Chief, outlined the facts of the German breakthrough at Sedan. Churchill listened to the analysis for a time and then asked in French where the strategic reserve was located: 'Ou est la masse de manoeuvre?' He received a single word in reply: 'Aucune.' None. For two hours the exposition went on, while Churchill sat beneath a perpetual column of smoke that he emitted from his cigars, and turned occasionally to gaze out of the windows where, as a lowly symptom of national despair, workmen were making bonfires of France's national archives. That evening Churchill telegraphed to his cabinet in London a request for ten additional fighter squadrons to fly to France, pointing out providently that they could if all failed be used to cover a withdrawal of the British Expeditionary Force, and at about 11.30 the cabinet telegraphed their approval. Churchill went immediately to Reynaud's flat to convey the news, and there, still crowned by clouds of cigar smoke, he kept Reynaud awake

The BEF withdraws : the troops disembark at a Channel port

until one o'clock in the morning regaling him with vivid pictures of how England would fight on if France were defeated, how they would starve Germany, burn her crops and forests, and destroy her towns, even if it meant Churchill himself moving to Canada to direct an air war fought by the New World over the ruins of the Old. Churchill slept at the embassy that night to the sound of air raids, and flew back to London the following morning.

He paid a second visit to Paris on 22nd May, but still no effective plan emerged for stopping the German advance, and French morale continued to evaporate. A few weak counter-thrusts failed, the surrender of the Belgian army appeared inevitable, and Lord Gort, commanding the BEF, decided to save his army by means of a fighting withdrawal to the sea at Dunkirk. On the night of 27th May the Belgian King duly surrendered his army, although the British, having foreseen such a move, managed to plug the gap which their capitulation created, and on the afternoon of 28th May the British Commander-in-Chief ordered his army to withdraw into a tight perimeter around Dunkirk.

On that day Churchill warned the House of Commons to prepare itself for hard and heavy tidings, after which he called to his room at the House all those members of the cabinet who were not actually in the small war cabinet, intending to put them fully in the picture. He explained the facts to them at length, and at the end of his address remarked quite casually: 'Of course, whatever happens at Dunkirk, we shall fight on.' Their reaction took Churchill entirely by surprise. The twenty-five or so men in the room erupted into an extraordinary expression of jubilation. They cheered, clapped, congratulated Churchill,

Some of the hundreds of small craft which voluntarily took part in the Dunkirk evacuation are towed up the Thames after their heroic mission

patted him on the back, and made it abundantly clear that they were determined to fight on with him until they and their country were totally destroyed. Churchill recognised at that moment that his parliamentary colleagues endorsed his unshakeable resolve to fight, and accepted him wholeheartedly as their leader.

In the meantime the troops retreating to Dunkirk were forming a perimeter in good order, and the ships which the Admiralty had requisitioned in readiness were beginning, by the night of 26th May, to take off the first of the evacuating force. In addition to the large ships which operated in Dunkirk harbour, an amazing force of nearly 400 small craft – pleasure boats, lifeboats, Thames tugs, fishing vessels, barges, and almost anything that could cross the English Channel – collected together in the Channel ports and from there, in a spontaneous and entirely voluntary gesture, were sailed by their private owners and peacetime skippers to Dunkirk where they played a vital part in ferrying thousands of troops off the beaches to the larger ships lying offshore.

In the midst of this operation, on 31st May, Churchill flew to Paris for a third meeting with the French, where he found that morale in the high command had deteriorated still further. Some of the younger officers were now contemplating moving to Africa to continue the war from bases within the French Empire, but Marshal Pétain had been brought back on to the scene, and he was evidently accepting the adverse trend of events, while at the same time exerting a strong influence in this line of thought on those around him. Despite this growing defeatism Churchill again assured everybody that Britain would fight on to the end, but Pétain dismissed this with the remark that Churchill 'sang his usual song'.

The Dunkirk evacuation went on until the afternoon of 4th June, by which time, according to Admiralty records, the ships had taken 239,555

Marshal Pétain

men from Dunkirk harbour and 98,671 from the beaches, a total of 338,226 troops who would form the nucleus of a new army for the defence of the British Isles and ultimately for Britain's part in the invasion of Europe.

On that afternoon, Churchill told the assembled House of Commons the story of the Dunkirk evacuation. Following his customary policy of sticking as closely as possible to the truth about Britain's position, he attacked those who had referred to the evacuation as a 'defeat turned into victory', and made no concession whatever to the fact that the BEF had lost a thousand guns and all its equipment in the course of a 'colossal military disaster'. He told the House: 'We must be very careful not to assign to this deliverance the attributes of a victory. Wars are not won by evacuations.' But he went on to point out that despite this the Royal Air Force had gained a victory within the defeat in beating back the majority of the German bombers. He then predicted with great accuracy: 'May it not also be that the cause of civilisation itself will be defended by the skill and devotion of a few thousand airmen?'

He ended his speech with this passage, which merits quotation at length: 'Even though large tracts of Europe and many old and famous States have fallen or may fall into the grip of the Gestapo and all the odious apparatus of Nazi rule, we shall not flag or fail. We shall go on to the end. We shall fight in France, we shall fight in the seas and oceans, we shall fight with growing confidence and growing strength in the air; we shall defend our Island, whatever the cost may be. We shall fight on the beaches, we shall fight on the landing-grounds, we shall fight in the fields and in the streets, we shall fight in the hills: we shall never surrender; and even if, which I do not for a moment believe, this Island or a large part of it were subjugated and starving, then our Empire beyond the seas, armed and guarded by

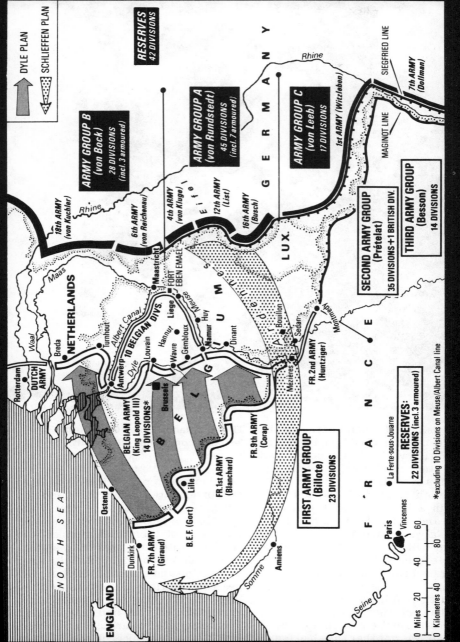

The opposing forces before the fall of France and the evacuation of Dunkirk

the British Fleet, would carry on the struggle, until, in God's good time, the New World, with all its power and might, steps forth to the rescue and liberation of the Old.'

That night, Churchill repeated those words in a broadcast to the British people, and just as his remarks to the cabinet a week earlier had drawn his political colleagues on to his side, so this speech brought about a remarkable transformation in the public. Until that time he had by no means secured their full support. Now their mood changed. They recognised in him an expression of their own unexpressed resolve. It was not that they had found a leader. The British, except for a

The commandos, men of Churchill's 'striking companies', in assault training

small minority of politically comitted supporters, are too cynical to look on heads of government as leaders. What they had in fact found was a spokesman, one of their own number who could put into words what they all felt, and by doing so could liberate their own action and energy. In Britain, the nearer a political figure gets to being 'one of us', the more certain his leadership becomes, and Churchill hit upon that fact early in the war. Perhaps he did so by accident. Perhaps he never realised it. By his background, unbringing, and character he could never be said to be in touch with the common man, and in fact at the end of the war there was ample evidence to show that he was not. But he managed to express, at that point in the war, the one sentiment on which the British people were united. While the French were prepared to capitulate and accept German domination for the sake of saving their beloved Paris from destruction, the British had a single and entirely different aim: they would sacrifice every brick laid down since the Romans invaded so long as they could keep the jackbooted German soldiers out of their lives. Churchill in fact struck the key

when he said 'We shall fight on th beaches'. If he would, they woul and at last the British people too him to their hearts.

One good indication of Churchill' character, and a guide to the reason for his success with the people o Britain, came on 4th June. On the pre cise day on which the operation to evacuate the BEF from the beache and harbour of Dunkirk was closing down, Churchill was already trying to get his country back on to the offensive. He wrote to General Ismay: 'The completely defensive habit of mind which has ruined the French must not be allowed to ruin all our initiative. It is of the highest consequence to keep

the largest numbers of German forces all along the coasts of the countries they have conquered, and we should immediately set to work to organise raiding forces on these coasts where the populations are friendly . . . An effort must be made to shake off the mental and moral prostration to the will and initiative of the enemy from which we suffer.'

At this stage, such exhortations could easily have sounded like so much hollow drum beating, but Churchill turned them into reality by an increased output of minutes on the subject which forced everybody around him into action. On 6th June he wrote a follow-up to Ismay proposing raiding parties into the enemy held coastline: 'The passive resistance war, in which we have acquitted ourselves so well, must come to an end.' He called for proposals for 'striking companies' which later became the 'Commandos', for landing craft to transport tanks on to enemy-held beaches, for a system of espionage along the coasts, for deployment of parachute troops, and for heavy guns to be prepared and mounted so as to fire across the English Channel.

Even after Dunkirk, Churchill continued with his efforts to keep the French in the war, and on 11th June made his fourth visit to France, this time to a château near Orleans. The government had abandoned Paris and were moving south, and had set themselves up temporarily in the comic-opera background of this castle, which provided only one telephone, incongruously located in the lavatory, and presented no accommodation whatever for Churchill's staff, who had to sleep in a train nearby. Churchill, in 'a real agony of mind and soul', explored all possible ways of persuading the French to continue the fight, but to Pétain a separate peace was the only way of saving his country from destruction by the

Charles de Gaulle, one of the few determined French officers

Germans. Most of the French leadership now backed Pétain: only Reynaud and a colonel called Charles de Gaulle saw any possibility of fighting on. Throughout these discussions Churchill was haunted by the knowledge that even with their enormous resources the British nation had not been able to make more than one tenth of the contribution to repelling the Germans that the French had made, and that it was the French and their country who were facing virtually all of the physical destruction. He felt shame and grief that his country had done so little: the only consolation was that it was not entirely his own fault.

Churchill's influence on the French affair was, as it turned out, negligible. As a last effort at preventing the collapse a scheme was hatched to combine the two nations in a common union, an idea which Churchill at first approached coolly, but which in the end he endorsed. He put the suggestion to Reynaud on 16th June, but nothing came of it. Reynaud resigned that day and was replaced by Pétain, who on 17th June sued for peace.

On 18th June Churchill spoke again to the House of Commons. In the course of this speech, having outlined the reasons for the lost battle in France, he pointed out the need for coming success in the air: 'I do not at all underrate the severity of the ordeal which lies before us, but I believe our countrymen will show themselves capable of standing up to it. Every man and every woman will have the chance to show the finest qualities of their race and render the highest service to their cause . . . Our professional advisers of the three Services unitedly advise that there are good and reasonable hopes of final victory. We have also consulted all the self-governing Dominions, and I have received from their Prime Ministers messages, couched in the most moving terms, in which they endorse our decision and declare themselves ready to share our fortunes and to persevere to the end. The Battle of France is over. The Battle of Britain is about to begin. Upon it depends our way of life. The whole fury and weight of the enemy must very soon be turned on us. If we fail, the whole world will sink into an abyss of a new dark age, made more sinister, and perhaps more protracted, by the lights of a perverted science. Let us therefore brace ourselves to our duties, and so bear ourselves that, if the British Empire and Commonwealth last for a thousand years, men will still say: "This was their finest hour".'

On that note, with the exception of the problem of the French fleet, Churchill's preoccupying concern moved away from France and became concentrated on preserving his own country from the impending invasion. In this respect he enjoyed the support of the British people, who were pleased to be able to get on with the war by themselves. Even King George VI confided in his diary his relief that Britain no longer had any allies to pamper with politenesses.

Britain's efforts to deal with the expected invasion fell into two distinct categories. At sea, there was little question of British superiority, at least until U-Boat operations developed to their full intensity. But on land and in the air there were grave doubts, and little time to remedy the deficiencies. In both these latter spheres, Churchill made it his business to be intimately concerned, and towards the end of June he began a series of visits to land defences along the east and south coasts of the country.

On such visits he travelled in his own train which was specially assembled for his purposes, and which served extremely well, particularly in the area of security: it kept Churchill, and the internationally important figures who accompanied him on later journeys, out of the public areas and away from hotels where they would have been vulnerable. It also helped preserve security of communi-

cations. A telephone engineer was among the substantial staff who travelled, and when the train pulled into a siding for the night he simply plugged a length of cable into a socket on the side of the Prime Minister's coach, unrolled a reel as far as the nearest telephone line, which often in Britain runs alongside the railway lines, and made the connection. A secretary then asked the local operator to connect him with a pre-circulated London number on a fictitious exchange called Rapid Falls, and the Prime Minister could be speaking to Whitehall by scrambler telephone within minutes. The train itself was assembled around the Prime Minister's personal coach, which had a large lounge in the centre, a bedroom and bathroom at one end, and an office for a private secretary and a typist at the other. A second large coach provided a lounge for the staff and other visitors, with the small compartments at the two ends available for use as offices to travelling VIPs. Behind these two coaches were a further coach consisting of first class sleeping accommodation and a shower; a passenger coach; and at the rear a van with a diesel generator for electricity. In front were a dining car, divided into two compartments for the main party and the staff; a kitchen car; a sleeping coach for the staff and crew of the train; and a luggage van. By using this mobile headquarters Churchill could not only save a great deal of time by sleeping and working while on the move, but he could observe his eccentric schedule with a minimum of disturbance to himself and inconvenience to everybody else.

On these early journeys Churchill quickly became familiar with the defence problem, and personally instituted many useful improvements.

The Prime Minister steps from an aircraft during a tour of east coast defences at the height of the Battle of Britain, August 1940

On one visit early in July he met general called Montgomery, in charg of a division near Brighton, who with no deference to the Prime Minister' position told him in outspoken term of the absurdity of failing to provide buses for his troops. Churchil immediately sent a minute to the Secretary of State for War, with the red ACTION THIS DAY label attached, pointing out the need for readily available transport, and suggesting that the buses which were still astonishingly plying for pleasure traffic on Brighton seafront should be used for the purpose.

The flow of minutes went on. What could be done to help people in the sea ports to build shelters in which they could stay during an invasion? What arrangements were being made to help people leave the invasion areas? Why was a highly trained Canadian division being sent to Iceland instead of being held ready to strike at an invasion force? Why were ships being allowed to move along the French coast with impunity? What arrangements were being made for the fast shipping and distribution of the half-million rifles bought from the United States?

While Churchill worked throughout the summer months of 1940 to galvanise the people into activity, and they in turn struggled to organise themselves and develop their strength for the anticipated invasion, there was fought out in the air over southeast England the conflict on whose outcome the success or failure of the entire invasion would depend. It was not what either Churchill or Hitler expected to be the Battle of Britain. Both of them, in the summer of 1940, expected that battle to be fought on land somewhere in England. But it was the nearest there ever was to a Battle of Britain, and therefore it took on that name.

The success of a projected German invasion, as Churchill and Hitler both knew, depended on control of the airspace above the English Channel.

Left and centre left : Anti-invasion devices are set up throughout southern England during the summer of 1940. *Bottom left :* A seaside shelter, sandbagged and wired for the people in the forefront of the invasion threat. *Below :* A Lewis gun emplacement is prepared outside the Admiralty as part of London's defences. *Right :* The Prime Minister at work in his train

The Luftwaffe in action. *Left :* A fuel storage depot at Purfleet burns after a bomb attack. *Right :* Aircrew return from a mission

August until about 7th September, during which time Reichmarshal Göring maintained a concentrated attack, according to sound strategic principles, against Britain's fighter stations in the south of England. In those two critical weeks Britain lost more than 230 pilots and nearly 500 fighter aircraft, and it is almost certain that if Göring had continued his attack on the stations themselves, he would have established mastery of the air in a short time, and could well have turned the course of the war. But whereas the British consistently saw the air battles in their strategic concept, and fought solely to maintain control in the air, Göring looked for more immediate results, and turned his attention away from the front line defences of the RAF to attack civilian population centres, notably London. The change occurred on about 7th September, and in the next few days the RAF was given enough breathing space to feed into the system its newly arriving machines and freshly trained pilots.

Churchill paid frequent visits to the fighter stations engaged in these battles, and on one particularly vital occasion, the afternoon of Sunday 15th September, he had driven down from Chequers to Uxbridge to look in on the control room of No 11 Fighter Group, which had twenty-five squadrons covering the entire south east of England below the Thames, which coincided exactly with the area of Hitler's projected invasion and included the approaches to London.

There, fifty feet below ground, Churchill and his wife sat in the operations room, built like a small theatre, with a map table on the floor and a blackboard on the wall opposite to the spectators' seats. The blackboard was divided into six columns, one for each fighter station,

While the British could with their immense superiority of sea power in the narrow seas be expected to destroy an invading force at sea, or at worst disrupt the organised supplying of such a force, they could only expect to do so as long as the navy was protected from air attack. Consequently, while energetic preparations continued at home to counterattack an invading force after landing, in the air the two sides fought to establish the conditions on which the success of such a landing depended.

The Battle of Britain opened on 10th July, when German aircraft began to attack British shipping in the Channel and continued with varying intensity for the next three months. The most crucial phase lasted from about 24th

with each column subdivided by squadrons, and each squadron column marked by a series of electric lights showing its situation: standing by, ready, available, in the air, in sight of the enemy, in action (a red bulb for this) and finally returning to base.

Soon after Churchill arrived information began to flow in from observer corps volunteers throughout the area, showing bombers approaching in large numbers. Churchill describes graphically in his memoirs the scene as the squadrons began to take off, and the series of lights came on indicating the various stages through which they passed. The tension in the room increased, and the level of activity rose as the busy plotters recorded the changing situation, while the

officers in charge, under Air Vice-Marshal Park, passed out orders in that calm, phlegmatic, efficient way in which the British specialise. As the battle reached its climax almost all the red lights came on, and all the bulbs showing reserves available were extinguished. It was obvious that every squadron in the group was fully committed, had 'shot its bolt' as Churchill described it, and most of its aircraft would now have to return to refuel, leaving no protection whatever in the air. 'The odds were great; our margins small; the stakes infinite' Churchill recorded. If the Luftwaffe at that point had attacked heavily the squadrons on the ground they might have destroyed Britain's fighter protection outright, but at this crucial

stage the discs on the map table below, operated according to the information fed by telephone from the innumerable volunteers out in the country, began to show a general movement of the German bombers to the east. The Luftwaffe had expended its own energy; the attack was called off; the all-clear sounded.

15th September had been the climax in the Battle of Britain, and Churchill had been present to see how his country, by the narrowest of margins, survived. That night the RAF's Bomber Command returned the attack, bombing shipping in Boulogne and Antwerp, and two days later Hitler postponed his plans for Operation Sea Lion, the invasion of Britain. He tried to resurrect the plan at several intervals later in 1940 and in 1941, but his best opportunity had passed. Britain was never again threatened with invasion with such inadequate defences, and the key to the inviolability of the islands had been mastery of the airspace above the Channel and the south of England.

In a speech to the House of Commons reviewing the progress of the Battle of Britain, which he later according to his usual practice broadcast to the nation, Churchill made the simple tribute which has passed into the body of immortal sayings: 'Never in the field of human conflict was so much owed by so many to so few.'

During September, the Battle of Britain gradually gave way to the Blitz; the Luftwaffe's fighter attack on the Royal Air Force defences declined, while the bomber raids on London intensified. After the first raid on London at the end of August, the Royal Air Force had retaliated by bomber attacks on Berlin, which of course gave Hitler the excuse to retaliate with further raids on London and subsequently other British cities. Churchill at this time saw the bombing attack against Germany as the

The RAF return the attack on the occupied port of Le Havre

73

Left: Lord Beaverbrook, friend and Minister of Aircraft Production in Churchill's government.

Göring extends his attack to British provincial cities *Below:* Manchester *Right:* Coventry.

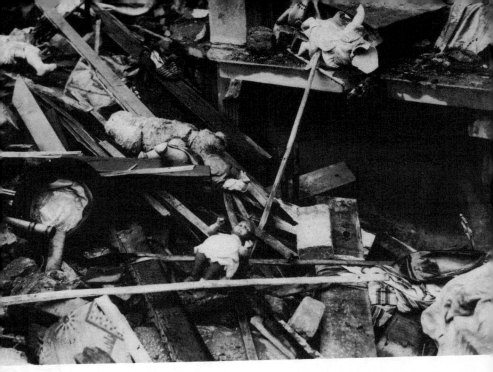

Wreckage and casualties during the Blitz on London

only means by which the British could mount an effective offensive against the Nazis, and draw them away from the attack eastwards which Churchill foresaw would follow once they realised that they could not invade the British Isles. He wrote to Beaverbrook, then Minister of Air-craft Production: ' . . . there is one thing that will bring him back and bring him down, and that is an abso-lutely devastating, exterminating attack by very heavy bombers from this country upon the Nazi Homeland.' Experience had not yet shown that such attacks only cement the resolve of the victims and increase their de-fiance, in Berlin as in London, and unless carried out to the ultimate point of total destruction are, in the modern jargon, counter-productive.

From the beginning of September to the beginning of November, every night for fifty-seven consecutive nights, waves of German bombers averaging 200 per night attacked London. During the first two weeks

they caused more than 10,000 civilian casualties. Arrangements had been made for the government to move away from Central London should air attacks become too dangerous, but no such move was ever seriously contemplated when the occasion arose. Until late in September Chur-chill himself remained at 10 Downing Street, where some ground-floor rooms had been reinforced to withstand a collapse of the building above. As the bomb attacks continued to hit the area of government buildings around Whitehall it promised to be only a matter of time before Downing Street itself was hit, and the building could certainly not withstand the direct impact of a bomb. Churchill and his entourage therefore moved to a more substantial building a few hundred yards away at Storey's Gate over-looking St James's Park and known as the Annexe. There rooms had been

prepared thirty-five feet below ground, with a war room, cabinet room, bedroom for Churchill, and modest living accommodation for the secretaries and for Mrs Churchill. The entire headquarters was protected by a shield of reinforced concrete, with fortified outer walls and a steel net over the central well. It was thought to be totally safe, although after the war engineers judged that a direct hit would probably have destroyed the building and all its occupants. At the height of the bombing in October, and before the fortifications of the Annexe were completed, Churchill bowed to pressure from his friends and moved temporarily to premises dug out eighty feet below ground at a disused underground station at Down Street off Piccadilly. There he was thought perfectly safe, but Churchill disliked having such a great degree of special protection, and towards the end of November he gave up that residence and moved back into the completed Annexe, where he and Mrs Churchill lived while in London until the end of the war.

Churchill in fact thoroughly enjoyed being in the centre of the attack, and viewed it with a large measure of fatalism. He described life at Downing Street at this time as being as exciting as a battalion headquarters, and few things gave him more pleasure than to go on to the Air Ministry roof where, he said, one could walk in the moonlight and watch the fireworks. He revelled in the atmosphere of the battlefield, and despite the admonitions of his staff he maintained an almost naive disregard for danger and approached the perils of war with a contemptuous air.

Inevitably, this outlook coloured his attitude to the people around him during the worst of the bombing. He quickly recognised that not all his compatriots savoured the atmosphere as he did, and ordered records to be

Mr and Mrs Churchill travel by Thames launch to visit the people of dockland

kept of the number of hours which civil servants spent away from their offices in the dugouts, and the records to be circulated among heads of departments. It soon became obvious that some people were spending more time away from work than they should, but as this embarrassing information was widely circulated, the time lost was rapidly reduced. He also personally put into effect a revised system of warnings which included an 'alert' as well as an 'alarm' stage, and thus prevented everybody rushing into their shelters as soon as an enemy aircraft appeared, whether it constituted a severe danger or not.

These entirely successful efforts to prevent officials from shirking contrasted with the approach he had to the ordinary people. In London, and in the provinces when their turn came to suffer the bombing, Churchill kept up an indefatigable round of visits to damaged areas. The majority of the bombs fell on the East End of London, around dockland, where rows of old vulnerable little houses stood cramped together, and the working class people who lived in them suffered the greatest loss. Churchill invariably found these people resilient, undaunted, and cheerful under the most adverse conditions, and despite the enormous casualties and damage to property they gave no thought whatever to the possibilities of surrender, or even, with the exception of their children, to any mass exodus from the city. Churchill quickly established a warm relationship with them. They invariably addressed him by his popular name 'Winnie', and approached him with none of the reticence normally reserved for holders of high office in the United Kingdom. Churchill's own words most vividly illustrate their attitude to him, in his description of a visit to a bomb-damaged area in south London: 'When my car was recognised the people came running from all quarters, and a crowd of more than a thousand was soon gathered. All these folk were in a

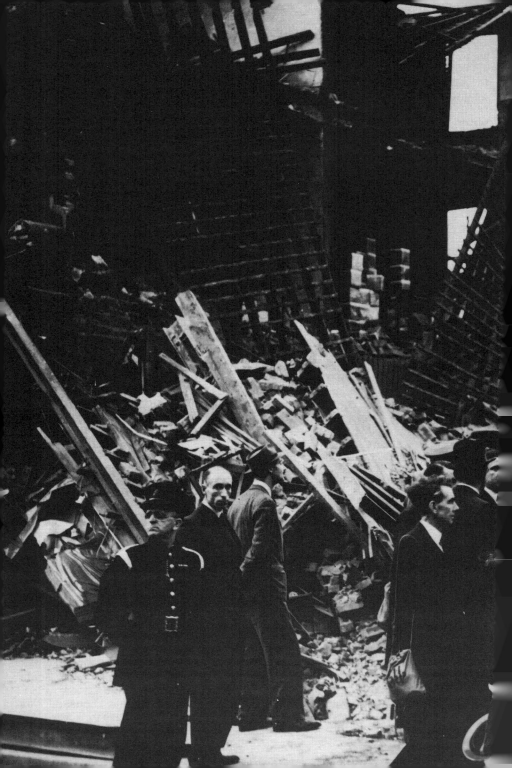

The ruins of London's East End

high state of enthusiasm . . . They crowded round us, cheering and manifesting every sign of lively affection, wanting to touch and stroke my clothes . . . I was completely undermined, and wept. Ismay, who was with me, records that he heard an old woman say: "You see, he really cares. He's crying." They were tears not of sorrow but of wonder and admiration.'

He left the scene to shouts of the crowd urging him to 'give it 'em back'.

Churchill was not, of course, in a position to have it all his own way during 1940. One particular experience stood out as a blemish on an otherwise favourable period, the unhappy expedition of the Free French Forces to land in Dakar on the West African coast. Churchill was at first a great supporter of this amphibious operation, designed to provide the Allies with a naval base and command of an important stretch of the Atlantic coast in Africa. Bad planning, serious security breaches, and inadequate intelligence undermined the chances of success, and Vichy French forces were able to reinforce their defences before the Allied expedition arrived off the town. The Allies were repulsed, with several important ships damaged, and before its conclusion Churchill took personal responsibility for calling off the expedition. He decided not to attempt to offer any explanation for the fiasco in parliament, and got away with that decision, and the best that can be said of the episode is that it provided invaluable lessons for amphibious operations in the future.

Churchill also during this period began to suffer the beginnings of what would later become a mounting campaign of political criticism. Robert Menzies, the Australian Prime Minister, wrote complaining bitterly of the Dakar incident. At home Mr Hore Belisha, a former War Minister and friend of Churchill's, attacked the government for not changing

British industry over to a total war effort. Then, when Neville Chamberlain resigned from the government with a fatal illness on 30th September, Churchill became leader of the Conservative party as well as Prime Minister. This appointment gave unnecessary ammunition to prospective critics: lifetime Conservatives could not forgive him his political past, when he had been a cabinet minister in the Liberal party. He also at this time carried out some cabinet changes, but certain sectors of the British press still attacked him for retaining in the cabinet some of the men who had supported the policies of appeasement at the time of Munich.

Overall, however, Churchill had enjoyed more than enough victories during the year to outweigh any unfavourable criticism. In September he had been able to announce to the House of Commons the Lend-Lease arrangement whereby Britain secured the use of fifty United States destroyers in exchange for leasing arrangements to the United States of property in the West Indies, Bermuda, and Newfoundland. This arrangement followed a lengthy and convoluted correspondence between Churchill and Roosevelt, and although the United States retained the nominal status of a non-belligerent, it was a definite step in the movement of that country towards active involvement in the war. And that was something which Churchill and Roosevelt both wanted. Britain had furthermore come through the Battle of Britain undefeated; London had survived the Blitz; and in December Wavell had begun a successful campaign against the Italians in North Africa.

The year had been one of the most remarkable in British history, accurately assessed by Churchill as 'the most splendid, as it was the most deadly, year in our long English and British story'.

He wrote: '. . . nothing surpasses 1940. By the end of that year this small and ancient Island, with its devoted Commonwealth, Dominions, and attachments under every sky, had proved itself capable of bearing the whole impact and weight of world destiny. We had not flinched or wavered. We had not failed. The soul of the British people and race had proved invincible. The citadel of the Commonwealth and Empire could not be stormed. Alone, but upborne by every generous heart-beat of mankind, we had defied the tyrant in the height of his triumph. All our latent strength was now alive.'

While the remainder of western Europe collapsed under the weight of Hitler's assault, Britain alone, despite a staggering deficiency in armaments, had resisted the apparently inevitable advance of Nazism. Britain had done so against the expectations of practically the entire world, largely through a combination of natural sea protection, the skill and exertions of a few hundred fighter pilots and their senior officers, and indomitable willpower.

In that last respect Churchill's own part was inestimable. He alone, by example and by exhortation, transformed a largely demoralised nation into one of inflexible resolution. And the principal weapon which he used was his remarkable oratory. In many respects, Churchill was indifferently equipped in the orator's skills. It is hard to think of him, for example, as inspiring a mass audience, rousing his listeners to a pitch of emotional fervour in the way that Hitler did. He was not even a natural speaker, as he freely admitted, and invariably worked for many hours on anything more than the briefest public comment. His speeches were composed in long and sometimes laborious sessions, well thought out and extensively polished, and typed in a special large typeface, phrase by

Hore Belisha (right) on the steps of the War office. Hore Belisha was a former friend of Churchill but one of the early critics of his government

A Matilda tank on the move, part of Wavell's successful December offensive in North Africa

phrase, on small sheets of notepaper. He called this system 'speech form', and since it had one phrase per line irrespective of brevity, it ended up looking rather like free verse. He continued the process of correction and composition right up to the last moment before rushing off to deliver the speech, but once he had begun speaking he did not depart from the text, but read it from beginning to end slowly and in sonorous tones. Nor was his delivery particularly elegant. He suffered all his life from a minor speech impediment which prevented his uttering the letter 's' correctly, and he never achieved the fluency and ease of tongue of, for example, the brilliant Welsh speaker Lloyd George, whose style in some respects his own so closely resembled. He was always apprehensive before a major speech, and never grew to enjoy using a microphone, despite his success as a broadcaster. According to Harold Nicolson, who served him as Parliamentary Private Secretary to the Minister of Information, he regarded it with such suspicion that he only agreed to broadcast at all after a great deal of persuasion.

Despite these drawbacks, he was devastatingly effective. His addresses to the House of Commons were almost always well-received and acknow-ledged by experienced members as being of the highest quality, and there is no doubt that in that assembly, which he loved and revered, he was an incomparable debater. Those speeches which he repeated to the nation nevertheless, according to those who heard both, lost a great deal in the transition, yet still they achieved immortality. The reason, without doubt, lay partly in their content. Churchill's message was exactly the message the British wanted to hear. He said precisely what they thought and felt, but being collectively inarticulate could not express. He also had the good sense to keep it straightforward and honest, and in his calm, ordered, unhysterical way, delivering rhythmic measured phrases with restraint but with total confidence, he hit upon a combination of rhetoric and simplicity which the British found irresistible. At the same time his tone was exactly right for the job: it was harsh, strident, even sinister, and there lay implicit in his voice a threat to those whom he attacked which sounded irrefutable. But perhaps most important, in Churchill's oratory as in any other speaker's, was his ability to reveal his own character, and the fact that the character he revealed was outstanding. It is beyond doubt that the qualities he showed in the speeches which he made in 1940 – the absolute courage, the total determination never to submit to the Nazi menace – pulled the British through the most serious crisis in their history.

At the end of that year, despite the few detractors, Churchill had built up a fund of good will and affection among the British people greater than that given to any other leader in modern times. It was well that he had done so. In the year 1941, when nothing seemed to go right either for him or for his country, he would have to draw heavily on that fund.

Destroyers provided by the US under the Lend Lease arrangements promoted by Churchill and Roosevelt

The Anglo-American Alliance

In January 1941 a flying boat touched down in Poole Harbour, on the south coast of England, carrying a particularly important passenger, arriving from Lisbon on the last stage of his journey from the United States. The man who came ashore by tender was a weak, frail little man of nearly fifty, the victim of a life-long succession of debilitating illnesses. He had been Secretary of Commerce in the United States government, and now served as a special adviser to President Roosevelt. Some observers regarded him suspiciously as having a sinister influence on Roosevelt. Roosevelt considered him, at this stage in the war at least, as an indispensable colleague, and had sent him to Britain as an emissary to make contact with Winston Churchill. Some time before the outbreak of war doctors had predicted that he would live for only a few weeks, and now this unprepossessing figure, well aware of his own physical weakness, was in England to carry out the vital job of being a middleman between the President and the Prime Minister.

Harry Hopkins spent that first weekend in close company with Churchill, and stayed with him all the following week, accompanying him on a visit to Scapa Flow, where he looked over the latest British battleship *King George V*, and subsequently making a

Harry Hopkins during his tour with Winston Churchill, January 1941

The Prime Minister's 'man Friday', Brendan Bracken, on Churchill's train in Canada

tour of Britain's war installations. The differences between the two men could hardly have been greater: Churchill robust, outgoing and extrovert; Hopkins frail and quiet, given to economy of utterance and caustic comment. But in the course of that week they developed a warm and lasting friendship based on a mutual appreciation of each other's qualities. And in the first few days Hopkins sent back a series of messages to Roosevelt in Washington which warrant quotation in some detail both for the light they throw on Churchill's personality, and because of their bearing on the relationship

between the two countries.

'Everyone tells me that he works fifteen hours a day and I can well believe it. His man Friday – Brendan Bracken – met me at the door – showed me about the old and delightful house that has been home of Prime Ministers of the Empire for two hundred years . . . Bracken led me to a little dining-room in the basement – poured me some sherry and left me to wait for the Prime Minister. A rotund – smiling – red-faced gentleman appears – extended a fat but none the less convincing hand and wished me welcome to England. A short black coat – striped trousers – a clear eye and a mushy voice was the impression of England's leader as he showed me with obvious pride the photographs of his beautiful daughter-in-law and grand-child.'

And later in the week: 'Dear Mr President . . . the people here are amazing from Churchill down, and if courage alone can win – the result will be inevitable. But they need our help desperately, and I am sure you will permit nothing to stand in the way. Some of the ministers and underlings are a bit trying, but no more than some I have seen. *Churchill* is the gov't in every sense of the word – he controls the grand strategy and often the details – labour trusts him – the army, navy, air force are behind him to a man. The politicians and upper crust pretend to like him. I cannot emphasize too strongly that he is the one and only person over here with whom you need to have a full meeting of minds. Churchill wants to see you – the sooner the better – but I have told him of your problem until the bill is passed. I am convinced this meeting between you and Churchill is essential – and soon – for the battering continues – and Hitler does not wait for Congress. I was with Churchill at 2 am Sunday night when he got word of the loss of the *Southampton* – the serious damage

HMS Illustrious suffers damage on her flight deck

to the new aircraft carrier (*Illustrious*) – a second cruiser knocked about – but he never falters or displays the least despondence – till four o'clock he paced the floor telling me of his offensive and defensive plans.'

And then: 'Your "former Navy person" is not only the Prime Minister, he is the directing force behind the strategy and the conduct of the war in all its essentials. He has an amazing hold on the British people of all classes and groups. He has particular strength both with the military establishments and the working people.'

Hopkins stayed in England long enough to hear the Prime Minister broadcast this message to President Roosevelt: 'Put your confidence in us. Give us your faith and your blessing, and under Providence, all will be well. We shall not fail or falter; we shall not weaken or tire. Neither the sudden shock of battle, nor the long-drawn trials of vigilance and exertion will wear us down. Give us the tools, and we will finish the job.'

The 'tools' in fact soon began to appear, for on 11th March Roosevelt put his signature to the Lend-Lease Bill, which Churchill called 'the most unsordid act in history'. It was however virtually the only item of encouraging news in that spring of 1941, which was otherwise notable only for the unvarying series of reverses which faced the British.

In the Balkans the arrival of German troops with overwhelming air support brought the almost immediate capitulation of Greece, and the Allies were forced to evacuate more than 50,000 men. In May the German air force mounted an attack on Crete, and another evacuation became inevitable: more than 13,000 troops were lost. In North Africa, a little known German general called Erwin Rommel had arrived and pushed the Allies back as far as Tobruk. At home, the bombing attacks on London were stepped up, reaching a climax on 10th May when more than 3,000 people were killed.

The Germans take Crete; infantrymen disembark from a Ju-52 transport aircraft, May 1941

In the midst of all these troubles, Churchill faced a new wave of disapproval which quickly became too serious for him to ignore. Military commentators criticised the dispersion of forces to Greece and Crete before gains in North Africa had been consolidated, and hit out at Churchill for deciding war strategy himself: responsibility for this, they felt, should rest on the General Staff or the commander in the field. The newspapers joined in the attack. *The Times* reprimanded Churchill for trying to run the war alone, and urged him to enlist the help of the keenest brains in the Empire. Other daily and weekly publications brought up a charge which had frequently been levelled at Churchill in the past, that he was deliberately surrounding himself with weak men. *The Sunday Times* called for a ruthless purge of elements in the

government which might impede the war effort, and for stronger, prompter, and longer-sighted ministerial changes on the civilian side of war planning than the minor changes which Churchill had made on 1st May.

On 6th May the dispute reached a political level, when in response to this tide of criticism, Churchill initiated a debate in the House of Commons aimed at securing a vote of confidence in his leadership, although it was technically cast in the form of a call for endorsement of the government's action in sending help to Greece. Many of the leading figures in the House spoke, including Hore Belisha who called for more mobility for the army, increased production of tanks, and air support as an integral part of the army. He also said: '... the Prime Minister has assumed a great and particular responsibility for strategy ... It might be said of him, as he said of Jellicoe, that he is almost the only man who can lose the war in an afternoon.' Lloyd George also made a powerful speech against the government, and particularly against Churchill, whom he attacked for trying to do everything himself: 'We have a very terrible task in front of us. No one man, however able he is, can pull us through. I invite the Prime Minister to see that he has a small War Cabinet who will help him – help him in advice, and help him in action.'

At the end of the debate, Churchill won his vote of confidence by a margin of 477 votes to 3 against, and left the House to an almost unprecedented storm of support, with members standing to make a lane for him and cheering him on his way. One newspaper, however, the *New Statesman*, attributed the demonstration of enthusiasm to the power of oratory, and made it clear that Churchill had still failed to allay the uneasiness about innumerable aspects of the war effort. Nor did the expression of support in Parliament serve to silence the critics for any length of time.

Winston Churchill's standing was not enhanced by further reverses which followed in June. On 15th June Wavell launched a counterattack against Rommel's forces in North Africa and failed completely. Churchill, whose relationship with Wavell had been deteriorating for some time, dismissed him and appointed in his place General Auchinleck, but before long relations with him began to deteriorate also.

The entire complexion of the war changed, however, when on 2nd June 1941 Hitler's armies moved eastwards and attacked Russia. The full significance of this step was not fully appreciated at the time, but it turned out to be one of the most far-reaching events in the course of modern history, and the consequences which flowed from it have shaped the pattern of affairs in Europe ever since.

An equally consequential event was

Rommel arrives in Tripoli

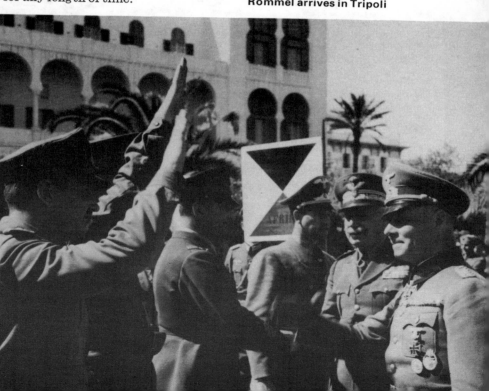

Left: Auchinleck, Churchill's replacement for Wavell, in North Africa. *Below and bottom:* Operation Barbarossa; the German armies march against the Soviet Union. *Right:* The Prime Minister travels to meet the President, on board the *Prince of Wales*, August 1941

the entry of the United States into the European conflict, and in August 1941 Churchill took a major step forward in his campaign to bring about that involvement. He met the President of the United States of America.

Churchill crossed the Atlantic in the battleship *Prince of Wales*, taking with him an impressive team led by the Chief of the Imperial General Staff Sir John Dill and the First Sea Lord Admiral Pound, and including Sir Alexander Cadogan of the Foreign Office and Professor Lindemann, now promoted to the peerage as Lord Cherwell. They set out with a destroyer escort on 4th August, but owing to foul weather in the Atlantic they were forced to choose between slowing their speed to keep station with the destroyers, or sailing on alone. To Churchill's delight they decided to

break with the escort and sail on alone at high speed, with frequent diversions to avoid reported U-Boats.

The venue for their meeting was an anchorage deep in the quiet and isolated Bay of Placentia on the Newfoundland coast, and when the *Prince of Wales* arrived there on the morning of 9th August the President's ship, the cruiser *Augusta*, already lay at anchor amid a small fleet of other American warships. As the *Prince of Wales* passed down the American lines, a band on each ship played the other country's national anthem, the two principles stood on the bridges of their ships, and a short time later Winston Churchill was climbing aboard the *Augusta* to present to the President a letter from King George VI. Then they immediately began the equally important tasks of consolidating the personal friendship which they had developed in their correspondence, and discussing the strategic questions which lay at the heart of their meeting.

The next morning, which was a Sunday, Roosevelt paid a return visit to the *Prince of Wales*, accompanied by his vast entourage of high ranking government officers and forces personnel, including General Marshall, Chief of the Army General Staff; General Arnold, Chief of the Army Air Staff; Admiral Stark, Chief of Air Operations; Sumner Wells, Under Secretary of State; and Averell Harriman, who had played a major part in securing the Lend-Lease Act.

That second meeting was the occasion for what Churchill saw as one of the most dramatic and memorable scenes of the war. The two leaders sat together; their staffs stood behind them, and sailors from the two countries stood together with their heads bared on the quarter-deck for a Christian service. They sang three of the most popular hymns they knew: 'Oh God Our Help In Ages Past', 'For

President Roosevelt pays his return visit to the *Prince of Wales*

Those In Peril On The Sea' and 'Onward Christian Soldiers'. It was not so much the act of religious witness which impressed the Prime Minister, but the expression of unity between the two nations: 'When I looked upon that densely packed congregation of fighting men of the same language, of the same faith, of the same fundamental laws, of the same ideals, and now to a large extent of the same interests, and certainly, in different degrees, facing the same danger, it swept across me that here was the only hope, but also the sure hope, of saving the world from measureless degradation.'

Thereafter their discussions ranged over the entire war area: the chances of the Russians avoiding defeat, British setbacks in Africa, the problems which the British Empire and other nations faced from the Japanese in the Far East. But there was no tangible result from the meeting. The nearest to it was a Joint Declaration, setting out the aims of Britain and the United States in both the war and the peace, which subsequently became known as the Atlantic Charter. It was written at the instigation of Roosevelt, who arrived at the conference with a clear idea that it should end with a manifesto, although Churchill was largely responsible for the text. He was always ready to lend his literary skills to such an endeavour, and after Roosevelt's initial suggestion he set to work on the first evening and dictated a provisional draught. Roosevelt made a few alterations on the following day, and others at the conference added their opinions, notably Lord Beaverbrook who had arrived by air. But the Atlantic Charter failed to shake the world. It made known 'certain common principles' of the two countries 'on which they base their hopes for a better future for the world', and expressed some general sentiments aimed at protecting the freedom of all states great or small in respect of their political and trading freedom, at establishing peace, and at pursuing disarmament. Churchill saw the declaration as of 'profound and far-reaching importance', amounting in ordinary times to a challenge which would imply warlike action. In fact, of course, no such action took place. The United States remained neutral, and Churchill was criticised on his return for failing to secure from Mr Roosevelt the declaration of war which so many observers had expected.

The true value of the Placentia Bay meeting, however, lay not in the declaration but in the relationship which the two leaders established. Heads of state are in the normal course of diplomatic affairs prevented by the nature of their positions from entering into close personal relationships with other heads of state, but these two men set up a warm informal friendship in which their own personalities overrode the restrictions imposed by their

offices. The friendship was to serve both men well during the next two years, until Roosevelt's declining health, and his developing views on a rapidly changing world scene, caused their relationship to cool.

Churchill for his part never lost sight of his idealistic vision of a united English-speaking world. Half-American himself, the son of the famous New York beauty Jenny Jerome, he felt that he had a special understanding of the American people. Perhaps he overestimated the common bonds between the two nations, but he consistently held to the ideal of a single Anglo-American force composed of the British Empire and the United States, enormously wealthy, overwhelmingly powerful, and inspired by fundamentally good intentions, working to abolish tyranny in Europe and protect the peace and integrity of smaller nations for all

time. Roosevelt admired the British, but did not share the partnership ideal to nearly the same extent. In his view, the influential figure in the future Europe was Stalin, and while Roosevelt concentrated on courting the Russian leader, Churchill in the coming years was forced to expend his energy on continual efforts to make Britain's voice heard at the international conference table. But for the time being Churchill cherished his ideal, and treasured the friendship he had established with Roosevelt as an essential element in it.

It proved to be a sustained feat of self-deception on his part, for the United States remained resolutely neutral for the rest of that year, and nothing Churchill or Roosevelt did or said could persuade Congress to involve that country in the war. Then,

Pearl Harbor

Churchill visits the United States, now Britain's ally, on board the battleship *Duke of York*

in December, the real impulse at last arrived, when Japanese aircraft attacked and destroyed a substantial part of the American fleet at Pearl Harbor. Churchill was at Chequers on the evening of 7th December, dining with the United States ambassador, John Winant, and with Averell Harriman. It seems extraordinary that neither the Prime Minister nor either of these two highly placed Americans received a report through official communications channels, but, like the Prime Minister and the British declaration of war two years earlier, these three only heard the news on the BBC radio bulletin.

Churchill was soon on the telephone to the White House, where Roosevelt confirmed that the attack had taken place. Characteristically, Churchill broke into one of his bursts of energetic activity, sending telegrams to national leaders in Eire, China, and

the United States, and setting his office at Chequers working to contact members of the cabinet and call a sitting of the House for the next day.

That night Churchill went to bed unashamedly thankful. 'So we had won after all', was his conclusion. Even at that early stage, with his premiership less than two years old, and with the fortunes of Britain and her Allies at their lowest, he regarded victory from then on as inevitably ordained. Congress would now have to change its mind and declare war. The vast resources and capabilities of the United States would be brought to bear, the Allies would constitute four fifths of the world's population, and however long it took victory was assured. Churchill recognised that there would be severe reverses, particularly in the Far East, but for him the declaration of war by the United States would mean that Britain had pulled through: the country and the British Empire were saved; the long history of the island race would not come to an end. He wrote: 'All the rest was merely the proper application of overwhelming force.'

That weekend was undoubtedly the climax of Churchill's war. It marked the fulfilment of his entire philosophy as a war leader. He had worked for this from the moment hostilities started, and now that his aim was achieved he could scarcely contain his joy and emotion. The next day he decided to travel to Washington immediately, secured the cabinet's approval in the morning, and wrote to the King in the afternoon. On 14th December, again leading a high-powered party which included Beaverbrook, Pound, and Dill, Churchill set sail in the Royal Navy's newest battlship *Duke of York*, again into such filthy weather that Admiral Pound decided to leave the destroyer escort which was keeping them to a slow speed and press on alone, hoping to cut through the U-Boat lanes unharmed. The voyage lasted for eight most uncomfortable days, with the ship battened down and the seas breaking over the bows, and no one allowed on deck, but Churchill kept everybody busy throughout studying the problems of the future of the war.

He himself spent a great deal of time and energy in creating a thesis of three papers on the course of the war. He dictated them fluently, but so slowly, he confessed, that they could have been written two or three times in longhand during the time that this process took. He conceived them, as was always his habit, as a means of marshalling his thoughts and clarifying his ideas on the subject under consideration, and he intended them primarily for circulation to the British Chiefs of Staff. On arrival in Washington however he gave copies to the President, who read them and asked if he could keep them. The first paper dealt with the need to occupy the entire coastline of North Africa, to prevent the link-up of Japanese and German forces, and to ensure the unhindered use of the Mediterranean by shipping; the second outlined the need to assemble and improvise enough aircraft carriers to clear and control the Pacific by May 1942; and the third specified as the ultimate objective the landing- of invincible Anglo-American armies to liberate the German-occupied territories in Europe, and nominated the year 1943 as the date for this 'supreme stroke'.

Although the events Churchill outlined failed to conform to the timetable envisaged, they did in fact evolve in the order which he set out. Churchill has often been severely criticised for deficient understanding of grand strategy, but in respect of this early analysis his views not only proved to be correct and accurate as predictions, but were totally acceptable to most of the staffs on both sides of the Atlantic as the correct procedure for bringing about the Allied victory. The only dissent came from Stalin, who from

In a lively mood, Churchill faces the cameras at the White House, dressed in his famous siren suit

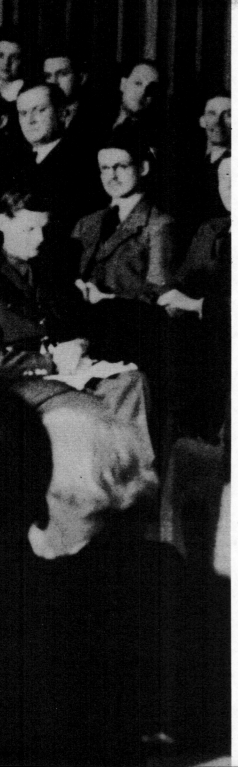

the date of Russia's entry into the war continued to press for a second front in Europe to relieve pressure on the Russian armies. His demands were based on entirely self-seeking interests, however, and were ultimately shown to be unrealistic: when the landing in France was eventually undertaken nearly three years after Churchill's exposition, the closeness of the issue demonstrated that an assault made earlier, and with weaker and less lavishly supported forces, would almost certainly have failed.

Churchill arrived in Washington on 22nd December, spent the first few days in consultation with the President, and celebrated Christmas at the White House. On Christmas Eve both he and the President addressed the crowds from the balcony of the White House, where Churchill gave a homely address in which he suggested that one night of simple festivities would be in order before they returned to the long and formidable tasks of war which faced them. 'Let the children have their night of fun and laughter', he said.

On 26th December he was invited to speak to the Congress of the United States, and it turned out to be one of his most successful speeches. 'I cannot help reflecting that if my father had been American and my mother British, instead of the other way round, I might have got here on my own', he told them, and with that opening completely won the support and sympathy of his audience. They re-remained on his side, laughing enthusiastically, applauding loudly, and rising to a climax of enthusiasm when, referring to the Japanese outrages, he asked rhetorically: 'What kind of people do they think we are?'

On 28th December Churchill took the night train north to Ottawa, where two days later he addressed the Canadian parliament, with a speech which proved equally successful. In it

The British Prime Minister speaks in Canada's House of Commons

he referred to the Vichy French who, he said, had been misled by their generals: 'When I warned them that Britain would fight on alone whatever they did, their generals told their Prime Minister and his divided Cabinet, "In three weeks England will have her neck wrung like a chicken". Some chicken! Some neck!' And with those remarks, it is fair to say, he brought the house down.

Later in that speech he took up again the theme which had featured in his Washington address, that of the fortitude of the Anglo-American peoples. 'I should like to point out to you that we have not, at any time, asked for any mitigation in the fury or malice of the enemy. The people of the British Empire may love peace. They do not seek the lands or wealth of any country. But they are a tough and hardy lot. We have not journeyed across the centuries, across the oceans, across the mountains, across the prairies, because we are made of sugar-candy.'

These speeches undoubtedly helped to cement the relationship between the British and the two north American nations, and paved the way for constructive progress in the talks which followed Churchill's return to Washington. One major fear among the British at this time was that the Americans would carry their isolationist attitudes into the war itself, and devote their main war effort to defeating Japan, partly as a revenge for the Pearl Harbor attack, partly to protect their vulnerable Pacific coast. The British view was that even if Japan were defeated, this would have little effect in reducing the threat from Nazi Germany which the United States would have to face should Britain fall, whereas if the United States joined in the war in Europe and eliminated the German menace first, the defeat of Japan would soon inevitably follow. But Churchill and the British Chiefs of Staff need not have worried. Roosevelt and his service chiefs agreed with the presentation given in Churchill's three papers. They also agreed on the formation of machinery for making their joint efforts work, with the creation of a Combined Chiefs of Staff Committee, consisting of the American Chiefs of Staff and permanent representatives of the British Chiefs of Staff, working normally in Washington, but prepared to meet at any other point in the world should the occasion arise.

The success of this meeting, following close on the United States declaration of war, had a profound personal effect on Churchill. During the preceding weeks there had been a number of noticeable changes in him. During the voyage across the Atlantic his doctor had observed that the weight of responsibility had visibly slipped from him. The tone of his life had changed. He was working as hard as ever, but his temper had softened, and the belligerent scowl which had previously seemed a permanent feature of his countenance had lightened. He looked a younger man, and the tired dull look had gone from his eye. The doctor, then Sir Charles Wilson and later Lord Moran, recorded that he had been frightened by the Churchill he had known in London, and wondered how long Churchill could go on in that way. Now he found him gay and voluble, sometimes even playful.

There was other evidence of the change in him. In a message transmitted on 10th December to the foreign secretary Anthony Eden, at sea on the way to meet Stalin in Russia, Churchill had listed the appalling series of setbacks that had occurred and the formidable problems they faced, but his mood was now so buoyant that he nevertheless ended with the sentence 'We are all having a jolly time here'. Then, while he was in the United States his assistant, Commander Thomson, had noted that he was disinclined to work on the final draft of his Canadian speech. He had settled on a rough outline, but nothing was on paper on the evening before the address was due to be delivered. In the event three secretaries together succeeded in getting the speech typed in time, although one page was left behind for further attention and the notes had to be brought to Churchill and slipped into place after he had begun to speak. Finally, although he was due to return home on new year's day, he felt so exhausted by the speeches and the strenuous work he had done that he readily accepted the offer by one of the President's assistants of the use of a holiday home he owned near Palm Beach in Florida. On the day before flying there, Churchill felt a pain in his chest while opening a window, and thought that he had strained his heart, but Wilson felt that he should nevertheless travel away for the holiday and on 4th January he flew south with General Marshall. He spent five days in Florida swimming and sunbathing, and enjoying by Churchill's standards a comparatively lazy time.

The fact was that Churchill was worn out. He had not had a real holiday for more than three years. The strain of the pre-war period, the political isolation, the loneliness as he stood out against prevailing opinion and predicted war, and then the enormous burden of leading the British nation struggling against the odds to survive in that war, had left him exhausted. And now that he was no longer leading the fight against Nazism alone, that exhaustion came to the surface. He could allow himself the luxury of feeling tired. In short, he began to let go.

At the end of 1941, however, this hardly mattered. Churchill's most important work was completed, and from this point his influence steadily declined. With the Russians beginning to be successful in the east and the Americans now participating in the war in the west, no single individual could any longer determine the course of events, least of all the leader of the least powerful of the three major allies. Churchill could afford to take his holiday; and it is well that he did so. At the end of it he was to return to Britain to face, in the early part of 1942, a further catalogue of disasters, and a chorus of personal criticism even more severe than that which he had faced at the beginning of 1941.

Lord Moran

In Pursuit of Strategy

On Christmas Day 1941 Hong Kong surrendered. In January 1942 the Japanese advance down the Malayan peninsular threatened Singapore, and in North Africa Rommel attacked and forced the British to evacuate Benghazi. There was ample ammunition for critics of the government, and now that Britain no longer faced invasion, many critics felt themselves freed from the self-imposed restraints of preceding years. When Churchill flew home, in his first Atlantic air crossing, he faced a mounting campaign of criticism of the government and his leadership, and even strong rumours in Westminster of his impending downfall. The newspapers were again leading the campaign: some complained that too little was being done to help the Russians, and called for the opening of a Second Front in 1942; others felt that the war effort was not being pursued with sufficient energy and organisational skill. In several sectors of the Press, as well as in political and public circles, the charge was raised again that Churchill had surrounded himself with insignificant figures. *The Times* published a letter recommending that Churchill should remain Prime Minister, but should change the structure and personel of the government. There were widespread suggestions that Churchill should work as a kind of figurehead, handing over executive power to somebody else. In view of this body of criticism, Churchill decided to ask the House of Commons for a formal vote of confidence in the government.

It was not the most subtle of political moves. Churchill failed to recognise that the criticism was not against him personally, but against the government he ran. His popularity was never seriously questioned, and it was perfectly obvious that he would win the vote he wanted. On the other hand, because the move was so transparently unsubtle, its effect could not be lasting. Churchill opened the debate

The Prime Minister tries a Sten gun

himself on 27th January, and spent more than two hours reviewing the war situation. He asked that the House should not press him to make scapegoats or to carry out short term measures which would not help the war effort, and he recalled that to his original promise of nothing but 'blood, toil, tears and sweat' could now be added 'many shortcomings, mistakes, and disappointments'. On the other hand, he told the House: '. . . it is because I see the light gleaming behind the clouds and broadening on our path that I make so bold now as to demand a declaration of confidence from the House of Commons as an additional weapon in the armoury of the United Nations.'

In the three days of debate that followed, Churchill's confidence was fully vindicated. All parties expressed their support for the government except the Independent Labour Party, and Churchill was grateful for their opposition. Without it no vote could have been taken at all. The party consisted of only three members; two of them were needed as tellers, leaving only one to register his protest, and the government ended with a majority of 464-1. The success of the vote had never been in serious doubt. Its failure would have brought Churchill's downfall, and no one in the country seriously wanted that, largely because of the absence of any obvious acceptable alternative Prime Minister. What the House wanted, in common with the Press and some of the public, was the opportunity to bring about an improvement, by a constructive campaign to improve the strength of the cabinet, and by preventing Churchill from trying any longer to run the war entirely by himself. His insistence on the vote of confidence had prevented that criticism from being effective, and it could only therefore be a short time before it began to mount again.

Churchill did, however, subsequently respond to the complaints to some extent by appointing a Minister of Production in the war cabinet, a

The Channel Dash ; *Scharnhorst* and *Gneisenau* break through the Straits of Dover

post which several speakers had suggested he should create, and by trimming the cabinet from eight members to seven and filling the posts with stronger men than previously.

In the midst of this fluid political situation at home, the problems on the fighting front continued to mount, and did so throughout the first half of the year. Rommel's offensive was proving successful, and in January he took Agedabia. On 12th February the German battlecruisers *Scharnhorst* and *Gneisenau* with the cruiser *Prinz Eugen* escaped from Brest and made their famous 'Channel dash' through the Straits of Dover into the North Sea. This was not the most significant of strategic losses, but the impudence of the German move, and the immunity of the ships to British attack, shook public confidence in the ability of the armed forces. Three days later,

on 15th February, news arrived that the Japanese had completed their advance down the Malayan peninsular and captured Singapore. In the Atlantic the U-Boat sinkings rose to alarming proportions, as the boats moved to the western Atlantic and began to sink undefended merchant shipping off the coast of North America. At the end of May Rommel launched a new attack evidently aimed at defeating the British armour and taking Tobruk. The battle wore on through the first two weeks of June, and by 14th June it was clear that Rommel had gained the initiative and that Tobruk was threatened with capture. Churchill telegraphed to Auchinleck stressing the need to hold Tobruk, in order to prevent any serious advance into Egypt, and Auchinleck replied that he had no intention of giving up the city. The battle was evidently not going well, but in London it was confidently felt that the defences at Tobruk,

The Japanese arrive in Singapore

which Auchinleck had spent several months preparing, would be sufficient to hold the base against the Afrika Korps.

That was the unhappy and uncertain situation, following a disturbing winter and spring, in which Churchill set out on his second visit to the United States, to settle with the President the general outline of future strategy, and to clarify the next stages in the development of the atomic bomb, the research for which was now proceeding under the code name 'Tube Alloys'.

Churchill, taking with him this time a small party, crossed the Atlantic in the flying boat which they had used in January. He felt that in view of the Middle East situation he should not be out of communication with London for any longer than necessary, and after twenty-seven hours flying time, a marked improvement on the full week he would have spent at sea, the Prime Minister touched down on the Potomac river. He spent that night at the British Embassy, and the next morning flew to Roosevelt's family home at Hyde Park, on the Hudson river.

Their early discussions were concerned primarily with the progress of Tube Alloys, and the two countries agreed to pool the results of their investigations so far, to transfer the

location of the research to the United States, where facilities could be made available which would not be vulnerable to German bombing, and to press ahead as fast as possible with the project. On 20th June the two men travelled overnight in the President's train to the capital, arrived at 8 am on the morning of 21st June, and after breakfast at the White House met again in the President's study for further discussions. There Roosevelt was handed a telegram, which he passed to Churchill without a word of comment. Churchill silently read the news which it contained: 'Tobruk has surrendered, with twenty-five thousand men taken prisoner'.

Churchill could hardly understand the message, and asked Ismay to telephone London for confirmation. It proved true. Yet another failure in a long line of British disasters had occurred, leading to the surrender of an enormous army (in fact thirty-three thousand men) to a German force approximately half as strong. To Churchill it was one of the heaviest blows of the war, a disgrace for the desert army and an indication, if the pattern was maintained, of even worse disasters to come in North Africa.

For the Prime Minister the affair

Tobruk falls, and British troops march into captivity

offered only one mitigating feature, that the President and his colleagues were entirely sympathetic. Their only concern was to enquire 'What can we do to help?' and Churchill, wasting no time, immediately asked for as many Sherman tanks as the Americans could spare to be shipped as soon as possible to the Middle East. The Americans responded immediately. General Marshall withdrew hundreds of tanks only recently issued to American armoured divisions, sent 300 Shermans, plus a hundred self-propelled guns, plus engines for the tanks to the Suez canal, and when a U-Boat off Bermuda sank the ship carrying the engines he ordered a second shipment to be sent out immediately. Churchill was overwhelmed by this generosity, and his embarrassment at having to ask for help was made all the more acute by the successes which United States forces were now enjoying in the Pacific. In May they had won the Battle of the Coral Sea, and in the first week of June they smashed Japanese naval strength in the theatre at the Battle of Midway.

During the final days of Churchill's American visit, news began to reach him of a new political crisis in England. The newspapers were again talking about a fall of the government,

Above : Consolation for Churchill after the surrender of Tobruk – American Sherman tanks supplied by General Marshall for the British forces in North Africa. *Left :* Churchill joins General Marshall to watch American army exercises in Carolina before returning from the United States to face a political crisis at home, June 1942. *Below :* The Japanese ship *Mikuna* sinks at the Battle of Midway, a turning point in the Pacific theatre war

there was widespread anxiety as a result of the fall of Tobruk, and a Conservative candidate had been decisively beaten in a by-election. On 24th June the new wave of attacks reached its climax when a distinguished and widely respected Conservative back-bencher, Sir John Wardlaw-Milne, tabled a motion in the House of Commons to the effect that 'the House, while paying tribute to the heroism and endurance of the Armed Forces of the Crown in circumstances of exceptional difficulty, has no confidence in the central direction of the war'. This was not the comparatively innocuous vote of confidence such as Churchill had initiated himself earlier in the year. It was a far more severe matter of a direct motion of censure, and from a leading member of Churchill's own party. Before he left the United States, Churchill predicted an opposition vote of no more than twenty if such a division was forced, and on 25th June he took off for Britain in a comparatively confident mood.

Shortly before the debate was due, Wardlaw-Milne offered to withdraw his motion of censure, but Churchill refused to allow him to do so. Speculation about the position of the British government ran throughout the world, and the only way Churchill could curb it was by a massive display of solidarity. The debate therefore began as arranged on 1st July. Wardlaw-Milne himself opened it with a powerful attack listing the government's shortcomings, but he suddenly destroyed his own effectiveness by making the suggestion that the Duke of Gloucester should be appointed commander-in-chief with absolute authority over all three services. Apart from the ineptitude of the suggestion, it was considered unforgiveable in the House of Commons to involve the name of a member of the Royal Family in a debate on a controversial issue, and Wardlaw-Milne's case immediately collapsed. After that, the opposition was vocal but

made no significant impact. Only Aneurin Bevan and Hore Belisha made effective speeches against the government. Bevan taunted them with the failure of British generalship, and suggested that five or six Czech, Polish or French generals then staying in Britain should be handed the leadership of the army until the British had learned how to do it themselves. He also attacked the class prejudice which permeated the officer ranks of the army, and told the popular story that if Rommel had been in the British army he would still have been a sergeant. He also suggested that Britain had only one successful general, a man called Michael Dunbar who had been a senior staff officer in the Republican army in the Spanish civil war and had won the Battle of Ebro, and who was at that moment a sergeant in a British armoured brigade.

Bevan was one of Britain's greatest political orators, but nothing even he said could swing any solid body of opinion away from Churchill's support. Churchill replied, at the end of the debate, with his usual masterly and lengthy survey of the war, and as usual he put himself in the hands of the House of Commons. He appealed for their support, and got it, with a division in his favour of 475 votes to 25. Churchill had survived his last major crisis of the war. The fortunes of the Allies were on the point of showing a marked improvement, and before long he would find himself, domestically at least, in a far stronger position.

Shortly after his success in the censure debate, Churchill decided to fly to Cairo to examine for himself the situation in the Middle East, and on the night of 2nd August he took off from an airfield in Wiltshire in a Liberator flown by an American pilot. It had been discovered that whereas the flying boat that he had used so far was unsuitable for the long flight, the Liberator could reach Cairo with only one stop at Gibraltar, and although it was an uncomfortable journey in the unheated converted bomber, they arrived in Cairo on the morning of 4th August. Churchill was delighted to be there. Not only was he back on the Nile, where he had spent some of the most exhilerating days of his young manhood, but he was away from London and enjoying again the atmosphere of the battlefield. He spent a week touring the area, meeting the officers and visiting the troops, and in the course of his travels came to the conclusion that he must alter the command structure in the region. He sacked Auchinleck, offering him instead a minor appointment covering a new command based on Persia and Iraq, and made General Alexander commander-in-chief in the Middle East. General Gott was given command of Eighth Army, but on the afternoon of 7th August he was killed when his aircraft was shot down. It was a blow to Churchill, but he lost no time in recommending to the war cabinet the appointment of a successor – General Montgomery.

As an interlude during his visit to Cairo, Churchill flew north to Moscow for a meeting with Stalin. It was essential, he thought, to avoid all possible misunderstandings through telegrams and intermediaries, and to visit Stalin in person to give him the news that there would be no second front in Europe during 1942. The party arrived on the afternoon of 12th August, and drove to a villa outside Moscow where they were to stay. There they were immensely impressed with the sumptuous conditions and luxurious hospitality with which they were greeted – 'totalitarian lavishness' Churchill called it – and that evening they went to the Kremlin to meet Joseph Stalin.

Churchill started their discussion

Churchill arrives in Cairo to sort out the military situation. Seated with him are Field-Marshal Smuts, General Auchinleck, whom he relieved of his command, and General Wavell

General Alexander, who took over from Auchinleck as Commander-in-Chief, Middle East

with an undeniably straightforward account of the situation, and of the reasons why he was forced to disappoint Stalin over the question of the Second Front. Stalin became depressed, and asked why they could not land a force of six divisions in northern France. Churchill countered that it would be folly to land so small a force, which would almost certainly be repulsed with irreparable damage to the prospects of a successful operation in 1943. Stalin accused the British of being afraid of the Germans, but admitted that he was in no position to insist on a landing in France if the British could not make one. Churchill then recounted the plans for the forthcoming operation in North Africa, Operation Torch, and Stalin warmed to the subject. This, Churchill explained, would be the Second Front, attacking the soft belly of the enemy (he actually drew a picture of a crocodile superimposed on a map of the Mediterranean) and it would take place in October of that year. Stalin listened keenly to this exposition, and Churchill went to bed feeling that he had made a good impression on the Russian leader.

The next day, unfortunately, he found that this was not so. Stalin spent two hours stating clearly his unfavourable views on the British. He accused them of being afraid of fighting the Germans, taunted them that they would not find it too bad if they tried it like the Russians, claimed that they had broken their promise to land an invading force on the Cherbourg peninsular, and told them that the supplies they had sent to Russia were only rejects. Churchill countered all these suggestions as they were made, and resorted to rather plain speaking to do so. In a heated fashion he told Stalin that he had travelled this great distance to establish good relations, and that at the moment there was no ring of comradeship in his attitude. Stalin seemed to appreciate Churchill's forceful manner, and even before the translator had made the

Above : The new and effective Middle East command ; General Alexander, left, and General Montgomery, right, the new Eighth Army commander. *Below :* Churchill arrives in Moscow ; Molotov holds open the car door

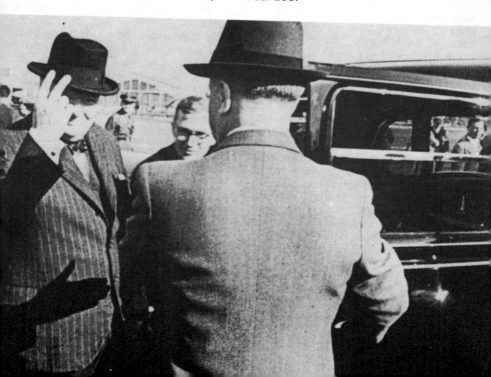

meaning of Churchill's words clear, said that he liked the Prime Minister's tone. After that Stalin's demeanor improved considerably. On the evening of 15th August there was an episode which enhanced their relationship still further. The British were due to take off back to Cairo at dawn the next morning, and at about 7 pm Churchill went back to the Kremlin to say goodbye to Stalin. After talking for about an hour Churchill was on the point of taking his leave when Stalin invited him back to his private apartment for some drinks, a suggestion which Churchill naturally endorsed. Together they made their way through the labyrinthine passages of the Kremlin to Stalin's home, and there over yet another protracted dinner, the two men settled the terms of their communiqué, and, even more important, Churchill felt that they had got on 'easy and friendly terms' and established a personal relationship which he thought would be helpful. At nearly 3 am Churchill, with a severe headache, left to go back to the villa, and from there to the airport where at 5.30am the Liberator took off for the flight back to Cairo. Churchill gratefully spent at least the first part of the journey asleep in the plane.

In Egypt, Alexander and Mongomery had taken over their new commands, and Churchill spent some days visiting the Eighth Army. Already there were striking signs of improvement in the Middle East. Under these two generals defensive arrangements were tightened, morale had improved immeasureably, aggressive spirit was beginning to prevail, and the men were well equipped and keen for the coming battle. The most notable examples of the new mood were the generals themselves: the calm, confident and gay Alexander, and the incomparable Montgomery, who made a great impression on the Prime Minister with his forceful and uncompromising nature. He was as autocratic and self-centred as Churchill himself, though

in entirely the opposite way. He neither drank nor smoked, and shunned the normal mess meals with his subordinate officers, preferring to take a frugal fare of sandwiches and lemonade alone in his staff car. He was also the only war leader with enough nerve to reject Churchill's exhausting late-night routine; he went to bed at ten o'clock every night whether Churchill was around or not. In Monty's caravan, at his headquarter at Burg-el-Arab, Churchill listened as Montgomery gave a lengthy and lucid outline of how he expected the coming battle to be fought, the moves Rommel would make, and the counters the Eighth Army would make to ensure victory.

This second part of Churchill's visit to Egypt was far happier than the first, so evidently happy in fact that the Chief of the Imperial General Staff had some difficulty in persuading Churchill to leave. He was eventually induced to realise that the Prime Minister hovering in the background while the battle was on would only be a nuisance, and on 23rd August he flew back to England, having cabled to the war cabinet: 'Everything had been done and is being done that is possible and it is now my duty to return home as I have no part to play in the battle which must be left to those in whom we place our trust.'

On 30th August Rommel mounted his attack, and it conformed precisely to Montgomery's expectations. The attack was repulsed, and the Afrika Korps took up defensive positions to wait for Montgomery's counterattack. Montgomery solidly refused to make one, and although Churchill could not resist urging him to greater efforts at the earliest possible date, he went on patiently building up his forces until he thought that the time was right to make the winning thrust. In fact Churchill had to wait for nearly two months, until 23rd October, before Montgomery began his attack, and although the outcome was uncertain for several days, and Rommel's troops mounted

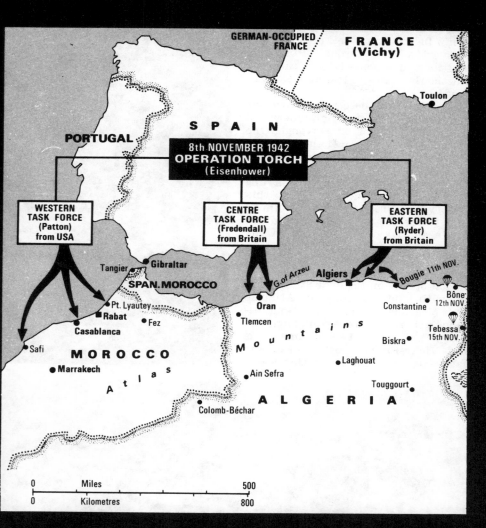

Operation Torch, the Allied landings in North Africa

a severe counterattack, the Eighth Army in the first week of November punched a hole through Rommel's positions and poured through it to put the German and Italian armies to rout.

Churchill was delighted. With the battle of El Alamein, Montgomery and Alexander had not only avenged the loss of Tobruk, they had also achieved the western Allies' first major land victory of the war. Churchill had planned to have the church bells rung throughout Britain to celebrate this victory, but Brooke persuaded him to wait to see the outcome of the other battle shortly to take place in the western corner of North Africa, when the United States entered the war in the west with Operation Torch.

That operation began on 8th November with landings along the Atlantic and Mediterranean coasts, and although there was some confusion, and heavy fighting between Americans and Vichy-French both at sea and ashore at Oran, the expedition was a

Above : The Prime Minister visits Montgomery's caravan headquarters.
Left : The first successful offensive ; British infantrymen examine a knocked out German gun after the battle of El Alamein. *Below :* Operation Torch ; an American gun is brought ashore

success. When Admiral Darlan arrived on the scene, he persuaded all Vichy-French forces to surrender and resistance ceased. Both Churchill and Eisenhower, the land commander, were subjected to severe criticism for their implicit recognition of the 'collaborator and traitor' Darlan, but Churchill rode out this criticism, and eventually it faded away after Darlan was killed by an assassin on Christmas Eve.

On the day that the cease fire took place following Operation Torch, Churchill said in a speech in the City of London: 'This is not the end. It is not even the beginning of the end. But it is, perhaps, the end of the beginning.'

In view of the complex network of strategic possibilities which the Allies faced now that they had gone on to the

Left : Admiral Darlan, two days before his assassination on Christmas Eve 1942. *Below :* Churchill and Roosevelt with French leaders Giraud and de Gaulle at the Casablanca conference. *Below right :* February 1943 : Churchill arrives in Tripoli during his extensive tour of the Middle East

offensive, it became evident that the President and Prime Minister should meet again to discuss the future course of the war. They asked Stalin to meet them also, but when the Russian leader refused to leave Moscow, they settled on Casablanca as the location for their conference. Churchill arrived there by air on 13th January 1943 and derived immense pleasure from being able to welcome Roosevelt, a day later, to newly won territory. Having got the conference under way, both Churchill and Roosevelt withdrew and left the Joint Staffs to solve the strategic problems: should they concentrate on mounting an attack across the Channel or continue their operations in the Mediterranean and build up from there the attack on Germany; if they were to press home their advantage in Africa with an attack towards Italy, should they move first towards Sardinia or Sicily? Churchill himself was in favour of an attack against Sicily. At one stage it was rumoured that he wanted to drop the cross-Channel plan altogether, but he assured Eisenhower that this was not so, while at the same time urging on him the wisdom of pressing home the advantage they had recently gained. In the end the Joint Planners agreed to the British view, and proposed to concentrate on the attack on Sicily, while at the same time building up forces in Britain for the cross-Channel attack.

At the end of the conference, Churchill persuaded Roosevelt to drive with him south to the city of Marrakesh, which Churchill dearly loved. There they enjoyed the sunset over the Atlas mountains, 'had a very jolly dinner', and at the end of the day both joined in a singsong. Roosevelt flew out the next morning, but Churchill stayed for two more days and began the only picture he ever painted during the Second World War. Following this conference, he made another extensive tour of the Mediterranean, visiting Cairo, Turkey, Cyprus, Libya, and Algiers, before returning home to present to Parliament an account of his recent activities and achievements. Then, on 16th February, he fell ill with an attack of pneumonia. His doctors had the greatest difficulty

in persuading him to rest, even in his sickbed, but eventually he agreed to see only the most important documents, and to fill the remainder of his time with a novel. He chose *Moll Flanders.*

In May 1943, with Tunisia captured and the Allies in total control in North Africa, the British again felt an urgent need to settle future strategy, and Churchill set off with an extremely large team for his third conference in Washington, code-named Trident. Since Churchill had only lately recovered from the attack of pneumonia, his doctors thought it inadviseable to allow him to cross the Atlantic by air, and with a team of more than one hundred he sailed from the Clyde in the *Queen Mary*, sharing the voyage with some 5,000 German prisoners of war. On 11th May they arrived off Staten Island, travelled by train to Washington, and began the conference at the White House at 2.30 on the following afternoon.

Roosevelt welcomed the British team to the conference, and expressed the view that their intention should be to bring to bear all their resources against the enemy, and that nothing should be allowed to stand idle. Churchill in his reply concentrated on the problem of Italy, and recited the long list of prizes which he thought would flow from the invasion and defeat of that nation: it would cast a 'chill of loneliness' over the German people; it might cause the Turks to make their bases available to the Allies to clear the Mediterranean; it would either cause the Germans to give up the Balkans or to draw off large forces from the Russian front to defend that area, and it would, by eliminating the Italian fleet, permit large scale naval forces to be diverted to the battle in the Far East against Japan. By this means, the Allies would also fulfil the Russian demand of a second front in Europe, and they would avoid the course which Churchill feared the most of keeping several divisions idle for several months until the invasion of northern France could be mounted.

Roosevelt replied to Churchill by pointing out some of the pitfalls of an occupation of Italy. It would, he felt, represent a drain on Allied resources which might better be used elsewhere, and at the same time would release large numbers of German troops for use elsewhere.

The differences of opinion which prevailed at the start of the conference were serious, and for a time it looked as if no compromise could possible be achieved. The discussions were heated, and the positions apparently irreconcilable. For Churchill, the principle of attacking Italy was central to his concept of strategy, the natural consequence of the successful clearance of North Africa and invasion of Sicily. The Americans, however, were at this stage still extremely suspicious of Britain's motives. They had long felt that the British were pursuing some kind of 'imperialist' philosophy in the Mediterranean, and they constantly suspected Churchill of being half-hearted about the attack on Germany through northern France. Most of the American officers concerned felt that the attack through northern France was the only operation worthy of any real effort or resources, and until the British were prepared to mount that operation, they considered it wiser to concentrate their effort against Japan. By the end of the conference on 25th May patient negotiation had reduced the gulf between the two sides, but nothing definite had been decided, beyond the general principle to concentrate first on the attack against the Axis in Europe before bringing their full resources to bear against Japan. The remainder of the final communiqué, much to Churchill's disappointment, consisted of an unexciting list of generalities, and omitted any mention of an attack on the Italian mainland as a means of exploiting their success in Sicily. The best Churchill could secure was a loose resolution from the Combined

Chiefs of Staff instructing the Commander-in-Chief in Italy to 'plan such operations in exploitation of "Husky" (the invasion of Sicily) as are best calculated to eliminate Italy from the war and to contain the maximum number of German forces.' The decision as to which operation should be mounted was to be left to the Combined Chiefs of Staff.

As it happened, all these difficulties and interminable discussion were made almost irrelevant by developments on the ground. Churchill planned to go to North Africa immediately after Washington, and he secured permission from the President to take with him General Marshall. He did not wish to appear to be exerting an undue personal influence on General Eisenhower, now named as Commander-in-Chief in North Africa, without a representative of the United States at the highest level. Accordingly the two men took off by flying boat on 26th May for Africa, where Churchill was 'determined to obtain before leaving Africa the decision to invade Italy should Sicily be taken'. In view of the Americans' previous stand, Churchill expected hard work in winning them over to his outlook. However it was Eisenhower himself who at their first meeting on 29th May volunteered unprompted the opinion that if they were going to knock Italy out of the war they should do so immediately after Sicily and with all the means at their disposal. The attack on Sicily would give a good indication of the kind of resistance likely to be encountered, and if it proved easy they should go direct to Italy. General Marshall still urged caution, and insisted that they should not formulate any firm plans until they saw how the battle in Sicily went, but by the end of the discussions, on 3rd June, he also had moderated his view, and was merely urging discretion in the selection of the right operation after Sicily. Churchill, after touring the area and meeting the victorious

troops, flew home in a far happier mood than he had been in when he left the unsuccessful and unhappy atmosphere of the Washington conference.

Within a short time rapid developments in the Mediterranean made it imperative for Churchill and Roosevelt to meet yet again and discuss the next stages in Allied strategy, and a meeting was hurriedly arranged with the code name 'Quadrant'. President Roosevelt suggested that Quebec would be an ideal location, and on 4th August Churchill began a second crossing in the *Queen Mary*. The principal outcome of Quadrant was an agreement to concentrate on the invasion of northern France as the prime long term objective, and to set a target date of 1st May 1944 for the operation. The Combined Chiefs also agreed to set up a separate South-East Asia Command, and appointed to the post Admiral Lord Louis Mountbatten, until then Chief of Combined Operations in Britain. The appointment of a commander for the invasion of northern France, Operation Overlord, was also settled. Churchill and the President had until that time agreed that the commander should be British, principally because the Americans had provided the commander for Operation Torch in General Eisenhower. By the time of Quebec, however, it had become obvious that the American armies would play a predominant role in the battle, and Churchill took it upon himself, evidently to the President's relief, to suggest the appointment of an American commander. Ostensibly this reasoning lacks conviction: Eisenhower had commanded in North Africa despite the preponderance of British troops, and Churchill had gone to great trouble to warn the House of Commons against complaining about the choice. On that principle he could legitimately have claimed his right to the British commander, but he evidently recognised the possibility of acrimony, and would let nothing

impede the fulfilment of his dream of total and perpetual Anglo-American cooperation. In coming to this decision Churchill was forced to betray his promise to General Brooke, to whom he had already offered command of Overlord, and although Brooke took the news with dignity, the decision was nevertheless a'crushing blow' to him.

A notable feature of the Quebec conference was the continuing dissention among the Allies, worse now even than it had been in Washington. At one point the discussions of the Combined Chiefs of Staff became so heated, and their disagreements so critical, that the conference promised to break down altogether. Perhaps the Combined Chiefs and their advisers

together formed a committee that was too big to be anything but unwieldy: more probably the presence of their advisers prevented the chiefs from expressing their views with their customary open frankness, or from conceding points since this might be construed as weakness by their subordinates. The only way they could escape from the dilemna was by dismissing their advisers from the meeting, and sitting down without them to thrash out the problems among themselves. One participant said later that they had 'really let their hair down', and afterwards they were able to move forward towards agreement.

These problems in Washington and Quebec were, however, only the early symptoms of discord, and from this time on it was Churchill's distressing experience to have to watch an increasing decline in Anglo-American relations, and a steady deterioration in his own personal and deeply cherished understanding with President Roosevelt.

Left: A pause during the Quebec conference, with his daughter Mary.
Below: Cairo, November 1943, and Churchill is embarrassed by the presence of General and Madame Chiang Kai-shek

The symptoms of disintegration really began to show when the two men met for the fifth major conference of the year, and the first at which all three main Allied leaders were present, at Teheran in late November and early December 1943. As a prelude to the conference, Churchill and Roosevelt agreed to meet in Cairo for preliminary discussions before flying on to Persia to meet Stalin. Without asking Churchill, Roosevelt invited Molotov, the Russian Foreign Minister, to attend their discussions, which inevitably would have inhibited progress. Molotov in fact refused to attend, but only because he learned that Roosevelt had

also invited Chiang Kai-shek, the Chinese leader, and the redoubtable Madame Chiang. Their presence proved an even greater hindrance, as Roosevelt insisted on giving priority to discussions of Chinese affairs, and ignored the proposed western front in France which was the main purpose of their meeting. Even on their own domestic affairs the Chinese delegation were so badly briefed and ill-informed that significant discussion was almost impossible.

When the leaders flew on to Teheran, on 27th November, the ill-feeling which Roosevelt's actions had begun to generate was intensified. Because the American embassy was some distance

from the Soviet embassy, where the discussions were to be held, Stalin invited Roosevelt to move into a villa in the Soviet embassy grounds. This step would solve the security problem presented by daily journeys through the streets, and Roosevelt quite sensibly agreed. But Stalin then proceeded to disrupt the prevailing diplomatic equilibrium by visiting Roosevelt a few minutes after he moved in. The Russian leader's genial good nature during this informal visit confirmed Roosevelt's view that Stalin was more favourably disposed towards him than towards Churchill, and Roosevelt came to the conclusion that he could 'handle' Stalin. His

determination to court Stalin was in fact so strong that on the morning of their second plenary meeting he declined an invitation to lunch with Churchill on the grounds that Stalin might think that the two western leaders were 'ganging up' on him and hatching schemes behind his back. Churchill took this rebuff well, and hid his distress behind the mildly humorous claim to being host for dinner the following night on three counts of precedence: that he was the oldest and alphabetically first; that he was the head of the longest established government, and that it would be his birthday anyway. He was in fact sixty-nine. Nevertheless Roosevelt, despite his 'ganging up' theory, had no hesitation in holding separate meetings with Stalin.

When it came to discussions of strategy, the isolation of the British leader and the apparent cohesion of views between the Russians and Americans was clear. At one session Roosevelt, who generally took the chair at these meetings, invited Stalin to comment on what operation in the west would be most helpful to the Russians. Stalin replied that he was against any dispersal of forces in the eastern Mediterranean. This was a natural point of agreement between the United States and the Soviet Union. Both were against any further involvement in the Mediterranean, the United States because they still suspected Churchill's intentions in the region, the Russians both because they wanted eastern Europe free of western influences, and because they genuinely thought that diversionary operations in the area might lead to an excessive commitment of troops who might prove impossible to disengage for the decisive operation in northern France. At later sessions Stalin pressed strongly both to know

The Big Three meet for the first time. The atmosphere seems cordial, but dissention among the Allies began here at Teheran

Canadian and British officials confer during the Prime Minister's visit to Quebec

the date of Overlord and to hear the name of the commander, at which point only, he maintained, would he really believe that the western Allies were serious about the operation. The month of May 1944 was eventually specified, but Roosevelt declined to name the commander, which was a subject still giving him a great deal of thought. A detailed examination of the record shows that Churchill was never, as the other two suspected, anything less than fully enthusiastic about the Overlord plan, but he did make the greatest possible efforts to hold off the operation until the required forces, particularly landing craft, could be assembled in order to avoid the humiliation of a major defeat. In the meantime he kept up the pressure for other operations because he could not tolerate the thought of large numbers of battle-proven troops being kept idle for several months until the main invasion could be mounted.

After Teheran, Roosevelt and Churchill returned to Cairo for brief discussions arising out of the meeting, and it was there that Roosevelt disclosed his appointment for the Overlord command; he could not spare George Marshall, and was giving Eisenhower the job. After Roosevelt's departure on 7th December Churchill stayed on in Cairo for four more days and then took off to visit Eisenhower's headquarters in Tunisia and subsequently Alexander's and Montgomery's headquarters in Italy. Churchill had in recent weeks been suffering from persistent colds, and in Teheran had almost lost his voice. Now he was feeling tired. As they flew to Tunisia, a confusion in landing orders forced his plane to put down on a deserted airfield. Churchill got out of the aircraft, and sat for a time in the cold early morning wind, hunched on his official boxes which had been piled out of the aircraft ready for a car journey. His doctor noticed that he was sweating and looked grey in the face, and that he

was slow in getting back into the aircraft. When he reached Eisenhower's villa he collapsed into a chair, did little work that day, and complained of a pain in the throat. He had already told Eisenhower that he was at the end of his tether and could not go to the front until he had recovered his strength. The next morning he had a high temperature, and an X-Ray examination showed a patch at the base of a lung. For the second time in a year, he had pneumonia.

Several specialists were flown out from London, and Mrs Churchill also arrived to be with her husband. His doctor clearly feared for Churchill's life, and Churchill himself sensed the gravity of his illness. His daughter Sarah, who was flying with him on this trip, records that on the first night of his illness he woke to see her standing beside his bed with a troubled look on her face, and said to her: 'Don't worry, it doesn't matter if I die now, the plans of victory have been laid, it is only a matter of time.''

He later prided himself on never letting go his control of the conduct of affairs, and on thwarting the efforts of his doctors and nurses to keep work away from his bed, but there is no doubt that he suffered severely with a raging fever. He stayed in bed until a few days before Christmas, by which time he was strong enough to get up and attend a Christmas Day Conference with the military chiefs in the Mediterranean, who turned up in force, Eisenhower, Alexander, Wilson, and Tedder among them.

Early in January Churchill flew over the Atlas mountains to Marrakesh to convalesce and recover his strength, before returning to the rigours of the English winter. At the suggestion of General Eisenhower he and his family stayed in a villa as guests of the United States Army, and there he established a routine of working in bed in the mornings, and going out on painting expeditions in the afternoons, taking a picnic lunch. He was still weak and complained of feeling tired, and at

times he could not take more than a few steps away from the car. On one occasion, during an uphill climb along a goat-track, his progress halted completely and his companions were forced to help him up the last few steps with the aid of a rope improvised from a tablecloth. But despite his condition he maintained throughout his stay a steady stream of visitors, including President Benes of Czechoslovakia, General de Gaulle, with whom he took the salute at a parade of the local French garrison, and the Pasha of Marrakesh. After two

Churchill, quickly recovering from his attack of pneumonia, meets General de Gaulle for a review of French troops during his convalescence at Marrakesh

weeks of comparative rest, Churchill flew to Gibraltar, went aboard the battleship *King George V*, and sailed for Plymouth. In the middle of a winter rainstorm he took the train for London and there, less than two hours after his arrival, Churchill was at his place in the House of Commons for question time. He had been absent from England for two months.

The Years of Failure

The year 1944, and the remainder of the war during 1945, were for Churchill dominated by two major concerns: the decisive landing on the continent of Europe; and the intricate problems of foreign policy involved in shaping the postwar world. Operation Overlord was, of course, despite a worrying hiatus before the breakout from the bridgehead, an almost unmitigated success, and led ultimately to the defeat and destruction of the German armies in the west. By contrast, in the field of foreign policy the period was one of continual frustration for Churchill, which in terms of the influence he was able to exert on the course of events must be counted one of almost total failure.

In the month before D-Day, Churchill spent a great deal of time on an exhausting tour of the units about to take part in the invasion. He enjoyed getting out and meeting the men who were going to take part, both the commanders and the troops themselves, but there were moments of strain. At one point the autocratic Montgomery refused to allow the Prime Minister to discuss with his staff the question of large numbers of vehicles included in the plan, on which subject Churchill had made several caustic comments. Generally, however, the preparations for the invasion proceeded smoothly, and Churchill's main concern, once the planners had handed over responsibility to the soldiers, was to fix the best place from which to see the invasion. He decided that he would go on one of the ships in the bombarding force, but General Eisenhower promptly attempted to veto that idea. Churchill pointed out that the American general had no right to determine the composition of any ship in His Majesty's Fleet, and that if Churchill decided to sign on as a *bona fide*

Churchill watches German troops firing during the Allied attack on the Gothic Line in Italy, August 1944. It was the nearest he got to the enemy during the Second World War

member of a ship's company the general would not be able to prevent him going. King George VI heard of Churchill's plan, and said that he also wanted to go along, a suggestion which Churchill was willing to put to the cabinet for approval. Before he was able to do so however the King thought better of the idea and said that it would be too great a risk for either the Sovereign or the Prime Minister to be removed from the scene at that point. He stressed that his anxieties would be increased by thought of losing Churchill's help and guidance at that point, and felt that the right thing for those at the top to do was remain at home and wait. This extraordinary and somewhat juvenile discussion went on for several days. The King argued that if it was not right for him to go, then it was not right for Churchill to go. Churchill considered that the risk was negligible. The King's adviser said that he understood that no subject could leave British soil without the King's permission, implying that Churchill could be thwarted by this means. Churchill countered that he would be in one of His Majesty's ships and technically still on British soil. The King's adviser replied that the ship would be outside territorial waters. Finally the King himself wrote to Churchill pleading with him to reconsider, and ending with an appeal that he should not let his personal wishes lead him to depart from his own high standards of duty to the state. Churchill was forced by this to cancel the plan, but only under protest. It was not the first time, nor would it be the last, that he had caused problems by his desire to see the battlefield for himself, a desire which many people considered tiresome and childish. His own view was that a commander sending men to their deaths might need the comfort of sharing in a small way their risks: his experience in the First World War had shown him that commanders should try from time to time to see the conditions and

Eisenhower takes Churchill on an inspection tour of troops

aspect of the battle for themselves, and he had seen many grievous errors made through the silly theory that valuable lives should not be endangered.

Churchill was in the end compelled to stay in his map room and wait for news of the invasion, and it was not until the third day after D-Day that he could take off for his first visit to the front in France, and even then bad weather prevented his aircraft from landing. On the next morning he sailed in a destroyer, and at last set foot on the European continent, when he visited Montgomery at his caravan headquarters five miles inland, in the company of Smuts, Brooke, General Marshal and Admiral King. On 20th July he was back in France touring the battlefield, continuing the tireless round of foreign travel which lasted throughout the war, and in which he covered scores of thousands of miles

by every conceivable form of transport. On 11th August he visited Italy, where he met Marshal Tito, leader of the partisans in Yugoslavia. On 14th August he visited Corsica to watch the mounting of Operation Dragoon, the landing on the French riviera, and sailed in a destroyer to watch the preliminary bombardment. Churchill had done his best to stop the operation taking place at all. It had been agreed at the Teheran conference to land in the south of France either one week before or one week after Overlord in the north, to draw off German defences from the main landing. The shortage of landing craft had made it impossible to keep to that timing, and Churchill now considered the operation a waste of resources. It would be better, he reasoned, to concentrate on exploiting the success in Italy, and moving towards Austria, or at least to land the divisions on the Biscay coast to be a more direct help to Eisenhower in the north. Both Roosevelt and Eisenhower refused to accept

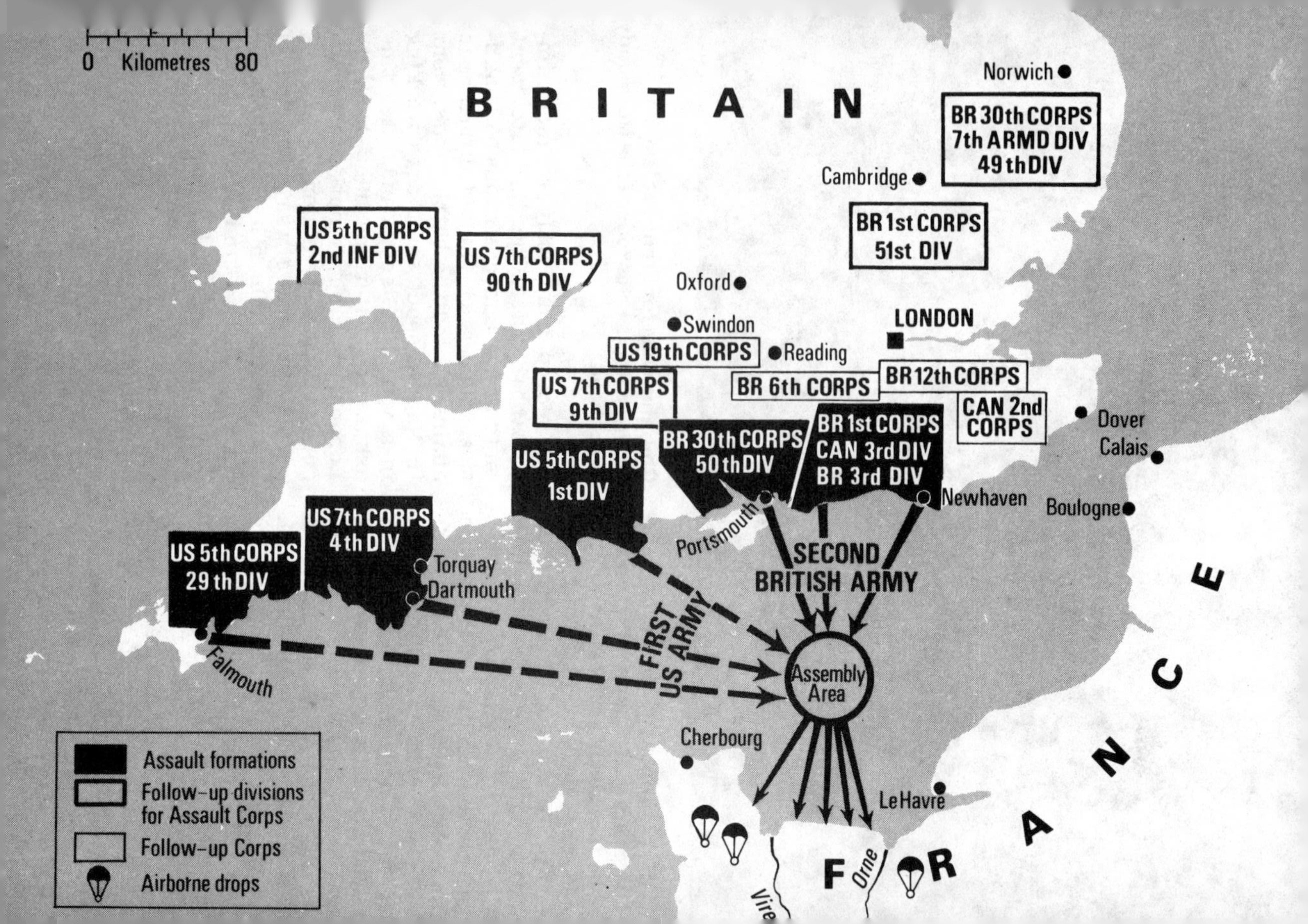
0 Kilometres 80
BRITAIN
FRANCE
Norwich
Cambridge
Oxford
Swindon
Reading
LONDON
Dover
Calais
Boulogne
Newhaven
Portsmouth
Torquay
Dartmouth
Falmouth
Cherbourg
Le Havre
Vire
Orne
BR 30th CORPS
7th ARMD DIV
49th DIV
BR 1st CORPS
51st DIV
US 5th CORPS
2nd INF DIV
US 7th CORPS
90th DIV
US 19th CORPS
BR 6th CORPS
BR 12th CORPS
CAN 2nd CORPS
US 7th CORPS
9th DIV
BR 30th CORPS
50th DIV
BR 1st CORPS
CAN 3rd DIV
BR 3rd DIV
US 5th CORPS
1st DIV
US 7th CORPS
4th DIV
US 5th CORPS
29th DIV
SECOND BRITISH ARMY
FIRST US ARMY
Assembly Area
Assault formations
Follow-up divisions for Assault Corps
Follow-up Corps
Airborne drops

Churchill's proposals, however, and the operation duly took place more than two months behind its originally planned schedule, with undistinguished results. Now that it was taking place, Churchill regarded it as a duty despite his objections to lend his support to the landing, although he spent a miserable day and had to comfort himself with reading a novel during the voyage back to Corsica.

On 17th and 19th August he visited General Alexander, the commander in Italy, and General Mark Clark, in command of the United States Fifth Army, who were both exceptionally depressed at losing a large proportion of their men to what they agreed was a mere sideshow in southern France. Both felt that they had been forced to sacrifice the chance of a decisive thrust north and east to take the prize of Vienna, which would have had significant effects on the pattern of the post-war world. Now they were limited to a holding action against potential German reinforcements be-

Churchill sails for France at last, and (right) makes a brief tour of the Normandy beachhead

ing moved from Italy to more important theatres. Churchill later went on to Rome to meet various personalities concerned in Mediterranean affairs, visited the battlefronts, went to Naples, spent some days working in a villa at Sienna, and after this exhausting interlude flew back to London, where he promptly went down once again with penumonia.

This time there was no period of recuperation. On 5th September he travelled to Scotland again with his Chiefs of Staff to board the *Queen Mary* for his sixth conference with President Roosevelt. They met in Quebec, and enjoyed the least exacting and for Churchill most pleasant meeting of the series. The only point of any real issue was the part Britain would play in the war after the end of hostilities in Europe, in order to bring about the defeat of Japan. Churchill sensed some hostility to British and Empire participation in the Pacific theatre, and was anxious to avoid the accusation later that Britain had failed to help the United States, after the United States had come to Britain's aid earlier in the war. He was also concerned that Britain should take part in regaining their rightful possessions in the Far East, and not have to wait until the United States handed them back at the conference table. Churchill asked Roosevelt for a definite undertaking about using the British fleet in operations against Japan. Roosevelt replied that he would like the fleet used wherever and whenever possible, but Admiral King, who was openly hostile to British participation, did his best to smother the plan, pointing out that the question was then being actively studied. Churchill returned to the topic immediately, and insisted on a direct answer. The offer had been made, he stressed: was it accepted? Yes, said

Roosevelt, it was. Apart from this minor altercation, the conference continued as it had opened 'in a blaze of friendship', as Churchill described it, and on 17th September Churchill left Quebec for a short visit to the President at Hyde Park before sailing home.

By this time Churchill's main concern in the war was moving out of the sphere of battles and their conduct altogether, and away even from the area of strategy, and into the field of statesmanship and international politics. On 30th August his friend Smuts had written to him: '. . . do not let strategy absorb all your attention to the damage of the greater issue now looming up.' In this field Churchill might have been thought to be in a position to make a special contribution, and his experience and opinions to be worthy of deep consideration. In fact, the political decisions and recommendations which he was to make during the remainder

of the war showed far greater grasp and assurance than his military and strategic thinking had shown, yet his influence now was at its lowest, and his contribution, with the exception of a well-timed intervention in Greece, almost totally ineffectual.

The first major problem he faced was that of Poland, and it was principally in order to settle this question with Stalin that he asked his assistants, immediately after his return from the United States, to make arrangements for a flight to Moscow. Stalin indicated that he would be welcome, and the President, who was too heavily engaged in his election campaign to attend, endorsed Churchill's plan and sent good wishes for the success of the visit. He arrived in Moscow on 9th October 1944, and on this occasion, in informal matters at least, found the Russians so unexpectedly friendly that he remarked

Above: Mr Churchill meets Marshal Tito in Italy
Right: General Mark Clark, commander of the United States Fifth Army, who joined Churchill in condemning the invasion of southern France. *Far right:* The Prime Minister gets a warm reception during his visit to Corsica

that they had never before got so close to their Russian allies. But on the Polish question their discussions were singularly fruitless. The British government, which recalled with chagrin that they had originally declared war in the interests of an independent Poland, gave their support to the Polish government-in-exile which had taken refuge in London. The Russians had set up a Polish National Committee, the Lublin Poles, who would make no concessions whatever to Churchill's proposals for a compromise between the two factions in order to achieve a united Polish government. Despite further discussions no progress was made, and the problem remained unsolved. On some other questions the two leaders enjoyed a greater measure of agreement, especially that of the Balkans. At their first meeting Churchill put to Stalin the proposition

that the British should carry major responsibility for affairs in Greece, Russian interests would predominate in Roumania, and they would bear equal shares of responsibility for the postwar control of Yugoslavia. Stalin agreed to these proposals without the slightest hesitation.

After flying home on 19th October Churchill began making more plans to visit Paris. The Allies had now recognised de Gaulle's Provisional French Government, and de Gaulle invited Churchill to take part in the Armistice Day celebrations on 11th November. After receiving a hero's

The second Quebec conference ; Churchill goes sightseeing at the Citadel

Churchill visits Cherbourg, and gets a light from an enthusiastic French supporter

welcome in Paris, followed by several days of celebration, he returned to London to face yet another crisis. Civil war had broken out in Greece. In anticipation of a German withdrawal from Greece, the British had persuaded the nationalist guerilla movements to sign an agreement placing themselves in the hands of Mr Papandreou's Provisional Government, which in turn would place them at the disposal of the British commander General Scobie. When the time came the ELAS guerillas refused to do so, on 3rd December they clashed

with the police, and civil war broke out. Scobie ordered the ELAS guerillas to leave Athens and Piraeus, but instead of doing so they attacked the police stations and moved against the government offices, whereupon Churchill took direct personal control of the affair, and on the principle that 'it is no use doing things like this by halves' sent orders to Scobie to fire on the guerillas if he had to. His telegram ended with the sentence: 'We have to hold and dominate Athens. It would be a great thing for you to succeed in this without bloodshed if possible, but also with bloodshed if necessary.'

For this vigorous handling of the episode Churchill was subjected to one of the most severe campaigns of Press criticism of his entire career. He was widely accused of interfering in the internal affairs of a foreign country, of causing British troops to fight against the Greek people, and of trying to impose the Royalist regime against the will of the people. The American Press were as vociferous as the British, and had ample ammunition when Churchill's 'bloodshed' message to Scobie was intercepted and leaked to a columnist who published it in full. The American State Department under Stettinius issued a critical statement.

There was of course a heated debate in the Commons, and Churchill's contribution included a lecture on democracy: 'I say that the last thing that represents democracy is mob law and the attempt to introduce a totalitarian regime which clamours to shoot everyone who is politically inconvenient as part of a purge of those who are said to have collaborated with the Germans during the occupation. Do not let us rate democracy so low, do not let us rate democracy as if it were merely grabbing power and shooting those who do not agree with you. That

Christmas in Athens ; the Prime Minister is helped down from the armoured car in which he crossed guerilla-held areas of the city

is the antithesis of democracy. Democracy is not based on violence or terrorism, but on reason, on fair play, on freedom, on respecting the rights of other people. Democracy is no harlot to be picked up in the street by a man with a tommy gun. I trust the people, the mass of the people, in almost any country, but I like to make sure that it is the people and not a gang of bandits who think that by violence they can overturn constituted authority, in some cases ancient Parliaments, Governments, and States.'

This uncompromising speech helped to restore Churchill's political strength, but the fighting went on, and the position of the British troops in Greece became precarious. General Alexander was sent to Athens with a free hand to restore order, but the ultimate aim of a political solution appeared no closer. The government of Papandreou ceased to have any influence, and the only alternative seemed to be the establishment of a regent approved by the King of Greece in exile. The name of Archbishop Damaskinos was widely canvassed, but the king refused to accept his nomination.

Throughout December the crisis ran on, and Churchill realised that he would have to go and see for himself the situation in Greece, and in particular meet the archbishop. It was Christmas Eve when he finally took the decision to go, after he had spent the afternoon reading increasingly grave news in the telegrams from Athens. He ordered his aircraft to be ready to fly that night, abandoned a family Christmas party at Chequers to begin his journey, and after breakfast and a refuelling stop at Naples arrived at noon on Christmas Day in bitterly cold Athens. Alexander and Scobie, together with Harold Macmillan and the ambassador, came on board for a three hour conference with Churchill and the Foreign Secretary Anthony Eden, and from there they travelled in an armoured car, with the Prime Minister carrying his loaded

143

Colt revolver across his lap, through areas controlled by the ELAS guerillas to the port of Piraeus, where Churchill and his party were to stay aboard the light cruiser *Ajax*. Archbishop Damaskinos was summoned, and he impressed Churchill both with his commanding bearing and with his outright condemnation of the communist groups in the city. Together they arranged a conference for the following night at the Greek Foreign Office, which the guerillas were invited to attend. After some delay the guerilla leaders did indeed arrive at the conference, and to the background noise of gunfire nearby Churchill made an introductory speech urging them to come to an agreement which 'will restore Greece once again to her fame and power among the Allies and the peace-loving people of the world, will secure the Greek frontiers from any danger from the north, and will enable every Greek to make the best of himself and the best of his country before the eyes of the whole world.'

The British party then withdrew to let the Greeks get on with their deliberations, and went back to the British embassy to wait for news. The conference among the Greek leaders went on for several days, although Churchill flew home on the evening of 27th December, having given Damaskinos an assurance of British support, and undertaken not to remove the British army from Greece until the ELAS guerillas had agreed to a truce.

Back in London Churchill secured the acceptance by King George of Greece of the Archbishop's regency; Damaskinos himself ultimately succeeded in forming a government which excluded the communists; and early in January the civil war came to an end. Churchill had, by his insistence on decisive activity by the British troops, run a grave risk of a catastrophic involvement in the affairs of Greece, although the risk he ran was wholly successful. His firm handling, and the decisive effect of his inter-

Archbishop Damaskinos, whose regency Churchill secured

vention during his own dangerous, inconvenient, and uncomfortable visit changed the entire pattern of Greece's immediate postwar history, and Churchill derived intense satisfaction at having saved Greece, as he saw it, from the inevitable fate of Soviet-dominated European states.

After celebrating the new year at home, and on 3rd January flying to France for another meeting with his generals and a tour of the forward units, Churchill faced once again the problems of the international post-war settlement: the Polish question, the control of Germany after her defeat, the fates of the small nations which would fall under Soviet domination. It was obvious that another

than seven of the eight plenary sessions. First they attempted to settle the question of the frontier. Churchill indicated that the British would be prepared to accept the Curzon line as the frontier in the east, which was a considerable concession to Russia on the pre-war position, and in return he asked the Russians to make parallel concessions in ceding the ancient city of Lvov to the Poles. Stalin refused, and suggested that the Poles should be given territory in Germany by way of compensation. In the face of this disagreement the question of the frontiers was referred for consideration to the Peace Conference after the war. An even more intractable problem arose over the Polish govern-

summit meeting presented the only possible chance of achieving any lasting settlement, and Roosevelt and Churchill therefore made plans for a conference with Stalin in Russia. The Russians chose the Black Sea resort of Yalta, in the Crimea, as the location, and there, after a preliminary meeting between Churchill and Roosevelt at Malta, the two western leaders and their enormous staffs, amounting to several hundred people, arrived for the first meeting on 5th February.

The main point of discussion throughout the entire meeting was the question of Poland, which featured as a major topic at no less

Lavish celebrations at Yalta. The hospitality was as generous as ever, but the political discussions produced little agreement

ment. Stalin continued to back the Lublin committee, claiming the right in the interests of security to a government friendly towards the Soviet Union. Churchill tried to establish the rights of the Poles to free elections, and to break the deadlock by agreeing to an arrangement which Stalin suggested under which the Lublin committee would be accepted as the provisional government after its re-organisation to include members of the London government-in-exile, and free elections would be held as soon as possible.

The western Allies were heavily criticised over this agreement on the grounds that they had betrayed the interests of the Polish people, and Churchill faced further hostile attacks in parliament on his return home. The agreements must however be seen in the circumstances in which they were made. Roosevelt, by this time severely ill, rejected Churchill's suspicions of the Russians, and not only still thought that he could 'handle' Stalin, but deliberately allowed all his dealings with the Russians to be dominated by the desire of the United States government to enlist Russian aid in the war against Japan. Churchill was allowed no part in discussions on this topic, and the two other leaders came to an amicable agreement on the terms of the war in the Far East: the Russians would take part in the war, and in return would take control of territory lost to the Japanese in the war of 1904, together with the lease of Port Arthur and control of the Kurile Islands.

Churchill's reduced part in the Yalta discussions was based on his country's rapidly deteriorating position in world affairs. Britain had fought for longer than the other two Allies, had exhausted its reserves of

foreign · currency, and was on the verge of bankruptcy. Churchill knew this, and did not dare take any steps which would jeopardise the Anglo-American alliance on which so much in the immediate future would depend. He argued his point of view with force and eloquence, but he was working from an impossibly weak position.

Immediately after the debate which followed his return from Yalta, Churchill was in Europe again visiting both Montgomery and Eisenhower. At the end of March he was back, this

Churchill crosses the Rhine, and later inspects a damaged bridge at Wesel where he came under shellfire

time to witness one the climactic moments of the closing period of the war. He flew from Northolt airport near London on 25th March and at dawn the following morning was in an observation post at Ginsberg, looking out over the Rhine as the airborne troops flew overhead to join ground forces in the crossing of the last great natural defensive barrier of the German armies. He spent the remainder of the day touring the area, and the next morning, returning again to the Rhine, told Montgomery that he wanted to go across to the other side. Montgomery was generally most uneasy at having the responsibility of looking after the Prime Minister,

but on this occasion, since the battle had moved some distance forward from the river, he agreed. Some minutes later Churchill stepped out of a landing craft for his first walk on conquered territory in Germany.

During these spring months of 1945 the war in Europe moved rapidly towards Allied victory, but for Churchill the period that should have brought an increasing sense of triumph brought only an accelerating

Combined Chiefs of Staff, his intention to deploy the forces at his disposal in a move east to join forces with the Russian armies at the Elbe. Churchill complained, accusing Eisenhower of improper procedure in contacting the Soviet leader without reference to the Combined Chiefs or even to his deputy, Air Chief Marshal Tedder, particularly since the decision which he made involved more than a million British troops still in

Russian and American troops link up on the Elbe. It was not the meeting Churchill wanted

sensation of unhappiness and doom. In addition to the difficulties raised by the Polish question, Churchill found himself in the middle of a heated row over the strategy employed by General Eisenhower. On 28th March Eisenhower telegrammed to Stalin, direct and without reference to the

the field. Even more serious than the propriety of Eisenhower's action was the strategic thinking behind his decision to ignore the possibility of capturing Berlin, which Eisenhower now saw as of minor importance. Stalin inevitably was delighted with Eisenhower's view, and in his reply to the initial telegrams said that Eisenhower's intentions entirely coincided with Soviet plans. Berlin, he pointed out, had lost its former strategic importance, and the Russians were therefore planning to allot secondary forces in that direction. The United States Chiefs of Staff naturally backed Eisenhower both in the procedure and in the substance of the telegram. Churchill anticipated that this would be their reaction, and although he continued to argue the case both with the President and directly with Eisenhower, he was at this point in the war able to exert strictly military point of view, and the military view prevailed. Eisenhower stuck closely to his orders, which were to destroy the enemy's armies in the field, and ignored the political considerations which the British now saw as paramount. By 5th April the discussion over Berlin had gone on for so long and to such little effect that Churchill decided to call it off, and in a telegram to Roosevelt said that he now regarded

almost negligible influence on events.

Part of the reason for this was that Roosevelt had by this time become so ill that his guiding wisdom had vanished. His letters to Churchill were evidently composed by his military and political aids, and the understanding on which the two leaders had based their relationship no longer obtained. General Marshall, who became Roosevelt's principal voice in military affairs, spoke from the the matter as closed.

The episode was one more example of the weakness of Churchill's position in the late stages of the war. His reliance on the alliance with the United States, the desperate state of Britain's resources and the country's recognised inability to pursue the war for much longer, the minority position of British armies in the field, the existence of an American commander-in-chief, whose selection

Churchill had wholeheartedly endorsed, the fact that Washington thinking was now dominated by military personnel and not political figures, all these factors combined to make it impossible for Churchill to impose his view on events any longer.

One week after Churchill accepted the inevitability of the American decision, Roosevelt died. Churchill's first reaction was to fly to the United States to attend the funeral and to

at midnight on 8th May with the formal unconditional surrender of the last German forces in Europe. That morning, Churchill broadcast the news to the nation, speaking from the cabinet room at 10 Downing Street, then forced his way through the dense crowds in Whitehall to the House of Commons. There members greeted him with a rapturous ovation, and Churchill moved, in the words used at the end of the First World

President Roosevelt is dead, and the American scene changes dramatically

meet the new President Harry S Truman. He got as far as ordering an aircraft to stand by for the flight, but because of the pressure of events at home and Europe, his advisers persuaded him not to leave the country at that time. It was a decision he would shortly regret.

The war in Europe came to an end

War, that the House should adjourn 'to give humble and reverent thanks to Almighty God for our deliverance from the threat of German domination'. After a service at the church of Saint Margaret, Westminster, and lunch with the King at Buckingham Palace, Churchill came out on to a balcony in Whitehall to speak to the people. 'This is your victory', he told them. 'It is the victory of the cause of freedom in every land. In all our long history we have never seen a greater day than this . . .' During the course of that afternoon and evening the Prime Minister came out on to the balcony several times to talk to the crowds. One of his political opponents, Ernest Bevin, led them in a rendering of the song 'For He's a Jolly Good Fellow', and Churchill himself conducted them in singing 'Land of Hope and Glory'.

Both Churchill and the people of settling the international problems, in bringing about the defeat of Japan, and in bringing the soldiers home, even if the present coalition had to remain in office for another twelve or eighteen months. But the Labour leaders turned down this arrangement, and in the electioneering atmosphere running through the country in that summer it was impossible to preserve the political *status quo* any longer. After some discussion with his col-

Churchill and colleagues in the British government greet the jubilant crowds in Whitehall on VE-Day, 8th May 1945

Britain enjoyed those victory celebrations, but for Churchill two great problems remained. One was the perpetually distressing state of international affairs, the other a new one occasioned by the end of the fighting – an impending general election at home. Churchill at this stage wanted to carry on as Prime Minister. He felt that he had invaluable influence, knowledge, and authority which the country would do well to employ in leagues, Churchill decided on a June election, asked for an audience with the King to recommend that he should dissolve Parliament, and was invited as head of the majority party to form a 'caretaker government' until the election results became known.

The campaign which followed was

AND NOW—
WIN THE PEACE

VOTE LABOUR

one of the most remarkable of modern times. Both sides threw their efforts into the party contest with an energy and partisanship in total contrast to the spirit of cooperation that had prevailed during the preceding five years. Both sides indulged in a campaign of vilification and mudslinging against the other, and Churchill allowed himself to indulge in this campaign in the most disreputable manner. Despite a lifetime of political experience, and a professed relish for the party political contest, he fought the election with startling ineptitude. A great part of the public by this time saw him as some kind of father figure, almost a presidential leader above the struggles of the party battle, and Churchill would have been better advised to capitalise on this sentiment. Had he stood above the party in-fighting, he might have attracted the floating vote of many politically uncommitted electors by a demonstration of his undisputed authority and statemanship, to the benefit of his own party. Instead he chose to enter the battle, and did so with an outlandish speech which lacked all credibility and served only to benefit his opponents: 'I declare to you from the bottom of my heart that no Socialist system can be established without a political police . . . No Socialist government conducting the entire life and industry of the country could afford to allow free, sharp, or violently worded expressions of public discontent . . . They would have to fall back on some form of Gestapo.'

The reference failed to frighten anyone away from the Socialist party, which after all was the party of Mr Attlee, Mr Bevin, and Mr Morrison, all of whom had served the nation and supported Churchill in exemplary fashion during the course of the war. Whether Churchill's approach, or indeed any other aspect of the election campaign, decisively affected the outcome is

Labour's simple and successful appeal in the 1945 election campaign

open to doubt. Churchill himself ascribed a great part of the blame for what later happened to the fact that most of his own party's managers were still in the services, so that the party's organisational machine was severely run down, whereas the Labour party was able to call on the professional skill of the managers in the trades unions, most of whom had remained at home to run the war industries. Some commentators have looked for reasons in other areas, notably the effective campaign of the *Daily Mirror* in its appeal to its working class readership, as opposed to the ill thought out electioneering of Lord Beaverbrook's Conservative-minded *Daily Express*. It is impossible to measure the influence of these various factors with any degree of accuracy. Most probably, the millions of men and women who voted would have voted exactly as they did whatever the nature of the political struggle that preceded the election. Most probably they were voting, as that 'floating' section of the British electorate which can influence the outcome of elections have so often voted, for a change of government, for some new kind of political order which would put the war behind them and concentrate on the construction of a just and prosperous peace. They were voting not for the party which they thought would best run their country and conduct the remote business of international affairs: they were voting quite simply, for themselves, and in that mood on 5th July 1945 they went to the polls.

In order to allow time to collect the votes of the servicemen abroad, a delay of three weeks would follow before the sealed ballot boxes were opened and the votes counted, and in the meantime Churchill devoted himself once more to the problems of securing a lasting peace in Europe.

On the international scene Churchill was by this stage in the war almost totally obsessed with his fears about the Soviet menace, which in his view had replaced the Nazi menace and unless correctly handled might well lead to a Third World War. The Soviet advance threatened to install communist regimes in almost every country in central Europe, including Poland, Czechoslovakia, Hungary, Austria, Yugoslavia and Bulgaria. Only Greece appeared to be safe, and Denmark would ultimately be spared from Russian domination by a well executed thrust to the Baltic by Field-Marshal Montgomery's army. Churchill saw clearly that the problem could be dealt with effectively only by means of a direct confrontation with Stalin, backed up by effective strength on the ground in Europe.

Unfortunately this picture was complicated by a large number of factors. The main one, which followed naturally from the end of hostilities in Europe, was the natural concentration of the United States Chiefs of Staff on the war in the Far East. At that stage, still some weeks before the successful field test of the atomic bomb which changed the picture so abruptly, it seemed likely that the war against Japan might last for another two years, and in the light of this assumption the United States military hierarchy was desperate to enlist the support of the still powerful Soviet forces. Their approach was therefore coloured by the need to avoid giving offence to Stalin. The American chiefs still concentrated on the military aspects of the problem, and almost totally ignored the political and diplomatic consequences, and the difficulty was further compounded by the American political situation. Although Roosevelt had died, Truman in these early months, having arrived at the White House by way of the Vice-Presidency and without the support of a direct mandate from the electorate, was still slightly tentative in his approach. He was evidently anxious not to countermand decisions technically taken by his illustrious predecessor, and still had not developed a sufficiently strong hand to impose his will on the service chiefs.

Churchill's own relationship with the Americans added a further complication. His personal friendship and regard for President Roosevelt had been the basis of Anglo-American cooperation for the first four years of the war. On the other hand Churchill had, apart from informal encounters when both men had been in Roosevelt's company, never met the new President. He now wrote to Truman expressing the hope that he could come to London on the way to the coming summit conference. Truman replied, to Churchill's great consternation, that he could not do so in case Stalin should gain the impression that they were 'ganging up' on him, a remark which echoed earlier fears of Roosevelt's at Teheran. Churchill had no alternative but to accept this decision, but he was even further distressed when an emissary arrived in London to convey Truman's view that Truman himself should meet Stalin somewhere in Europe before Churchill arrived for the conference of the three leaders. At this affront Churchill sent a sharply worded note to the President laying down firmly that the British would not attend any meeting except as equal partners from the opening. He also outlined in one powerful paragraph the considerations which he felt should govern the approach to the Soviet Union: 'It must be remembered that Britain and the United States are united at this time upon the same ideologies, namely, freedom, and the principles set out in the American Constitution and humbly reproduced with modern variations in the Atlantic Charter. The Soviet Government have a different philosophy, namely, Communism, and use to the full the methods of police government, which they are applying in every state which has fallen a victim to the liberating arms. The Prime Minister cannot readily bring himself to accept the idea that the position of the United States is that Britain and Soviet Russia are just two foreign Powers, six of one and half a dozen of the other, with whom the troubles of the late war have to be adjusted. Except in so far as force is concerned, there is no equality between right and wrong. The great causes and principles for which Britain and the United States have suffered and triumphed are not mere matters of the balance of power. They in fact involve the salvation of the world.'

Truman accepted Churchill's remarks, and nothing more was heard of his suggested meeting alone with Stalin. Nevertheless, the Americans remained suspicious of Churchill's political involvement in the European scene, and continued to regard themselves as some kind of intermediary, or even arbiter, between the British and Soviet claims in Europe, with no special inclination towards either side. The clearest example of the divergence of views arose over the question of the withdrawal of Eisenhower's troops. Strict zones of occupation for the Allied nations had been agreed, and the advance of the western Allies had taken them up to 120 miles forward of the demarcation lines. Churchill, on the basis that the entire picture had been changed since the occupation zones were settled two years earlier, pleaded with Truman either to bring the date of the summit forward, or to postpone the withdrawal of United States troops from Soviet-designated zones until after the conference had taken place. Only in this way, he argued, would they be able to sit down at the conference table with any bargaining strength. Truman judged that a postponement would harm relations with the Soviet Union and therefore ordered the withdrawal to take place as arranged. On 1st July the British and American armies began the withdrawal to their own zones, pulling back on a 420-mile front by distances of up to 120 miles. As Churchill wrote: 'Soviet Russia was established in the heart of Europe. This was a fateful milestone for mankind.'

How far Churchill was to blame for this state of affairs is difficult to assess. Certainly he saw more clearly than any other statesman the trend of events in Europe, and he had done his best to avert them. The interesting question is whether he had tried to do this by the right means. Churchill undoubtedly felt that the personal approach to the President which had worked so brilliantly with Roosevelt would work with Truman, and it did not. He failed to notice that the conditions of decision making in Washington had changed, that both the civil and military staffs who advised the President had developed in strength during the course of the war, and that his personal influence on the course of events had diminished. It is possible that had he called a full scale conference, with his own chiefs of staff, he might have been able to impress upon the Americans the changing nature of the European situation; but their detachment from Europe, their need to enlist Stalin's aid in the war against Japan, and their suspicions of Churchill's political ambitions in Europe all predominated. The fact that he failed to recognise that his own personal influence was no longer a telling factor in international affairs must be counted a fault, even if his reading of the situation itself was unerringly accurate.

It was against this unpromising background that the three leaders came together at Potsdam, with no preliminary side meetings, for the last summit conference of the war. The conference lasted from 17th July until 2nd August, and for the western Allies was the most difficult and the most fruitless of them all. In their private meetings, and in the innumerable lunches and banquets in which everybody vied to impress the others with the hospitality their countries could offer, Stalin and Churchill developed even further the warm informal relationship which had been evident

Above left: The international statesman returns to domestic politics, and goes campaigning in his constituency at Woodford, Essex. *Left:* The Potsdam conference, totally fruitless from Churchill's point of view. *Above:* Churchill is absent. Attlee returns to Potsdam as Britain's Prime Minister, and only Stalin remains of the original 'Big Three' at Yalta. In official discussions, by contrast, their relationship almost completely broke down.

At Stalin's suggestion, Truman took the chair, and the discussions resolved themselves almost entirely into a debate between Churchill and Stalin. The main subject of their dispute was again Poland, and Stalin, knowing that he occupied the strongest pos-

sible position, made few concessions, and succeeded in evading all Churchill's attempts to pin him down to a definite commitment. On all the questions at issue – the Polish government, the frontier, the territories claimed from Germany – there were long and rambling discussions, but no solutions. Most of the issues were in fact referred to the Foreign Secretaries for discussion, which effectively put them on the shelf. And that is where most of them remained when Churchill flew back to London on 25th July to hear the results of the general election the following day.

That night Churchill slept badly, and just before dawn woke with a strong premonition that his party had been beaten. His mind dwelt for some

minutes on the consequences of his removal from office, the loss of power to shape the future, the waste of the experience and knowledge he had built up, but although he was deeply disturbed by these thoughts, he managed to get back to sleep and woke rather later than usual.

The centre of activity throughout that day was the map room, transformed temporarily into a political office with a tape machine to receive the results as they were announced, and a collection of blackboards to report the gains and losses, and present a running picture of the changing situation. Shortly after 10 am the first result was announced, a win for Labour. Throughout the morning the results came flooding in, and it was soon obvious that Churchill's premonition had been well founded: striking Labour gains were being reported throughout the country. Some notable Conservative members lost their seats: Duncan Sandys, Churchill's own son-in-law; Harold Macmillan; Brendan Bracken; Leo Amery; all important figures in the party. Half way through the morning the result came in from Churchill's own constituency at Woodford in Essex. The Labour party had respectfully declined to put forward a candidate in opposition, but an independent had stood, with a totally eccentric programme. Churchill polled 27,688 votes; his opponent the astonishingly high total of 10,488. The people in the map room ate lunch in an unhappy and strained atmosphere, and throughout the afternoon the results continued to show a Labour landslide victory, until by six o'clock a Labour majority was certain.

The shock was so brutal to Churchill, the verdict of the people at that moment seemed such an affront, that he could not stand the thought of remaining in office for a moment longer. He drove to Buckingham Palace, and at seven o'clock had an audience with the King, at which he offered his resignation and advised the King to send for Mr Atlee. When the final results were known Labour had amassed a huge majority in the House of Commons, with 393 seats compared with 247 for all other parties. Churchill's defeat was overwhelming.

It was some days before Churchill moved out of the Prime Minister's official residence at 10 Downing Street, but his work as Prime Minister was over. The frenzied pace of activity had died away: his concern with events had finished, and there is no doubt that he was deeply hurt and distressed, both by the decision of the electors and by the abrupt change in his own life. He told his doctor shortly afterwards: 'I get fits of depression. You know how my days were filled, now it has all gone. I go to bed about twelve o'clock. There is nothing to sit up for . . .' He was seventy years old.

He spent the next weekend at Chequers, but again the emptiness of the atmosphere depressed him. On the Monday morning he came back to London, read the evening newspapers in the afternoon, and that evening drove down to his home at Chartwell with his daughter Mary. The house had been closed since the beginning of the war, and the gardens had become overgrown and tangled. They walked through the gardens together and Churchill told his daughter that the house he loved was like a sleeping beauty. He decided to stay in the house that night, and next morning was out in the garden early, supervising the work of clearing away the nettles and weeds.

Although he was now Leader of the Opposition and due to play an active part in postwar politics for almost another two decades, that return home was symbolic of the end of the Prime Minister's war.

Winston Churchill was a private citizen again.

Mr and Mrs Churchill leave 10 Downing Street. The Prime Minister returns to private life

Bibliography

Action This Day edited by Sir John Wheeler Bennett
(Macmillan & Company, London)
The War That Churchill Waged by Lewis Broad (Hutchinson, London & New York)
A Thread in the Tapestry by Sarah Churchill
(Andre Deutsch, London; Dodd Mead & Company Inc, New York)
The Second World War by Winston S Churchill
(Cassell & Company Ltd, London; Houghton Mifflin Company, Boston)
Churchill in his Time by Brian Gardner (Methuen & Company Ltd, London)
Churchill, the Struggle for Survival, 1940–1965 by Lord Moran
(Constable & Company Ltd, London)
The War and Colonel Warden by Gerald Pawle
(George G Harrap & Company Ltd, London; Alfred A Knopf Inc, New York)
Churchill, Four Faces and the Man by A J P Taylor and others
(Allen Lane, The Penguin Press, London); published in the USA as
Churchill Revised (Dial Press Inc, New York)